ISRAEL
Yesterday and Today

A Photographic Survey of the Building of a Nation

ISRAEL
Yesterday and Today

A Photographic Survey of the Building of a Nation

Amiram Gonen

Photography: Duby Tal

MACMILLAN • USA

Graphic Design: Hayim Shtayer

Project Manager: Rachel Gilon

Piloting: Moni Haramati
Albatross Aerial Photography

To Rika, with whom I share the joy of landscape watching

MACMILLAN
A Simon & Schuster Macmillan Company
1633 Broadway
New York, NY 10019-6785

Copyright © 1998 by G.G. The Jerusalem Publishing House and Shlomo S. Gafni
39 Tchernichovsky St. • POB 7147 • Jerusalem Israel 91071

MACMILLAN is a trademark of Macmillan, Inc.

Library of Congress Cataloging-in-Publication Data

Gonen, Amiram.
Israel yesterday and today : a photographic survey of the building of a nation / Amiram Gonen.
p. cm.
ISBN 0-02-862585-4
1. Israel--History, Local. 2. Israel--Pictorial works.
I. Title.
DS126.5.G64 1997
956.94--dc21   98-5343
                                                                                                      CIP

Printed in China
10 9 8 7 6 5 4 3 2 1

Contents

Looking Back at Change

Changes recorded in history books can be exciting, thanks to our basic curiosity to understand how things were in the past and how they came to be what they are now. Looking at change through pictures collected over the years, however, can be a more exciting and even more joyful experience. We all enjoy following, for example, photos of the development of a baby into a fully grown adult, especially if the baby was ourself or someone we cherish and love. We enjoy browsing in car albums, tracing the changes in car models from what now seems the somewhat clumsy and outlandish designs of the early models to the elegant and dynamic shapes of contemporary ones. We are thrilled when finding our predecessors' old robes, tucked away in a forgotten closet, and comparing them with the fashionable clothes of today. We also enjoy examining an old photograph of a place we know or have an interest in — a building, a street or a view of a village or town — and are amazed at the way that place had looked in former years. We enhance this gratifying experience when comparing the old view with what it looks like now, by examining recent pictures and comparing them with the old ones photographed from the same point and at the same angle. It is even more enjoyable when we are given the opportunity to gaze at photographs taken periodically of the same place—at times in between. We can thus follow how a small house was extended and redesigned with much care and ambition only to find out from subsequent photographs that the enlarged house has been replaced by a high-rise building, leaving no trace of the original structure. Sometimes we are lucky to come across photographs that show entire sections of cities consisting of a large expanse of open space interspersed with a few lonely houses, and to find that later on, as portrayed by a series of similarly taken photographs, the fields were turned into built-up areas and the old, lonely houses gradually surrounded by a densely-built urban environment. Sometimes we are fortunate to find that a few of those old houses have survived up to the present, serving as a reminder of how things were once upon a time. To those of us who are ardent watchers of landscape transformation, such houses serve as a bench-mark for identifying

Jaffa Gate in the Old City of Jerusalem in the 1910s — with the clock tower.

the changes that took place between then and now. We are often astonished by the visual changes. It is difficult to believe that places we presently know are so different in pictures from the past. We are eager to discover the connection between the past and the present, to find some similarities and look for differences between the two points in time. This book addresses such curiosity and its resultant wonder and joy, in the context of a country's landscape, in the changing expressions of Israel over more than a century, since the beginning of intensive Jewish settlement and modernization.

The Historic Role of Photography We have to thank the inventors of the modern camera and some enthusiastic photographers for the fact that we can now follow clearly the transformations that have taken place in Israel. The country attracted some professional photographers who took it upon themselves to document vividly the way the country looked when the changes began and even some time before. Many of these photographers wanted to show the world outside — through their pictures — how the ancient cities and sites in the Holy Land looked. They focused on scenes connected with important personalities, places and events in the history of the country. The Old City of Jerusalem, of course, being the holy city for Jews, Christians and Muslims, attracted most of these photographers, who produced a wealth of photographic documents. They eternalized the views of the city in the early days of the second half of the nineteenth century, before everything began to change. Some early photographers traveled out of Jerusalem to record the views of the ancient cities of the country. Tiberias, with its breathtaking views of the Sea of Galilee, was at that time a small fishing town surrounded by old walls and the sea. Zefat, or Safed, was a dreamy town with its strip of Jewish and Arab quarters clinging to the slope of the mountain and hardly matching the important role of the city in

Jewish kabbalistic tradition. Nazareth, revered by multitudes of Christians around the world, was not much different in size in the mid-nineteenth century from the way it looked in antiquity. Much of the surroundings of its historic sites were set, over a century ago, in shabby poverty and rather poor conditions — a sight that moved the pilgrim and the occasional romantic tourist. Haifa, today a large port city and the metropolis of the north of the country, was nothing more than a port village then, second in importance to the historic maritime center of Acre, across the bay to the north. Along the coast, south of Haifa and Acre, only the port town of Jaffa amounted to anything that looked urban. The coastal plain around it, up to Haifa in the

Above: The Sultan's Pool near the Old City of Jerusalem served as a cattle market in the late 1880s. In recent decades it hosts open-air musical events. The Yemin Moshe neighborhood is on the right.

Below: The Sephardi synagogue on the southern outskirts of Tiberias in the early twentieth century.

north and Gaza in the south, was settled by villages and small towns. The Arab towns of Lydda (Lod) and Ramla were the only urban-looking ones between Jaffa and Jerusalem. In the middle of the nineteenth century, Jaffa thrived on the fact that it had been the coastal gate to Jerusalem and, indeed, many of its early photographers attempted to capture again and again port scenes of tourists and other travelers landing from an anchoring ship, using small boats manned by Arab stevedores. On the road from Jaffa to Jerusalem, the horse-pulled carriages passed through Lydda and Ramla, the main attraction there being impressive architectural remnants of much more heroic periods when Muslims and Crusaders had fought for control of

the land. Views along the dirt road, now a major highway, to Jerusalem, were occasionally documented in photographs by the early travelers as they were climbing the hills and mountains on their way to the Old City of Jerusalem. As the first Jewish settlements were gradually appearing in various places around the country, some photographers became conscious of the fact that a

Above: Jaffa, at the turn of the twentieth century, was the country's main port of entry.

Below: Gedera, one of the new Jewish moshavot in 1910.

significant change in the make-up of the country was looming. They sensed the value of recording the early beginnings of what heralded an overwhelming transformation of the landscape and the evolution of a new reality—of a growing presence of Jews around the country, and not only in the holy cities of the remote past. The first of the new Jewish settlements were called *moshavot* (colonies; the Hebrew plural of *moshava*). These were agricultural villages established in the likeness of European villages, with independent, private farmers who tilled their own land and maintained only a minimal level of cooperative economy. The early *moshavot* were largely established by religious Jews, most of them originating in Eastern Europe. As more and more *moshavot* were sprouting around the country, they too became the object of photographic documentation.

For instance, with the help of mid-1890s, we are now able to Hadera. In this *moshava* in the coastal plain, the first Jewish with malaria spreading in their

photographs taken in the retrace the beginnings of northern Sharon region on the inhabitants struggled bitterly midst from neighboring

swamps. We can also take a look at Rishon Leziyyon, a new Jewish colony southeast of Jaffa. There, a string of farmhouses was lined up on each side of the main street, facing the synagogue. This virgin view of Rishon Leziyyon can be compared with what has now become the main street of a city housing over a hundred and seventy thousand inhabitants. The same goes for places like Rehovot and Petah Tiqva; once tiny agricultural villages and now fully-grown cities with only a few vestiges of their rural past in some of their older streets. Many photographers later photographed the beginnings of the new Jewish neighborhoods to the north of largely Arab Jaffa, eventually known as Tel Aviv. Unlike Haifa and Jerusalem, where Jews lived in the same city with Arabs, sharing the management of municipal affairs under the guidance of the Ottoman and later the British rulers, Tel Aviv presented the first example of an up-and-coming new Jewish city, run by a Jewish-controlled local government. At the time, Tel Aviv was called the "First Hebrew City," to signify its modern and national character. Indeed, Tel Aviv became an important symbol of Jewish national revival, due to its urban expression. Therefore, photographers were anxious to record the emerging "Hebrew" landscape: Hebrew streets, Hebrew buses, Hebrew schools and Hebrew houses. The changes recorded in their photographs were swift. In a matter of one decade, through the 1920s, the garden suburb of Tel Aviv turned

The Herzliyya Gymnasium in Tel Aviv in the 1910s.

into a busy commercial hub in an urban environment. Many recently built detached homes, surrounded by green gardens, gave way to middle-rise buildings that housed families or commercial establishments. The rise of urban Tel Aviv as a fast-growing city that was built on sand dunes was one of the most rapid changes in the landscape that took place in the early stages of Jewish nation-building in the country.

Other photograph favorites in Israel were the various agricultural settlements based on varying degrees of cooperation: the *kibbutz* and the *moshav*. The *kibbutz* (*kibbutzim* in the Hebrew plural) is a communal settlement where all the economic functions, production and servicing are communally owned and run and where individual households are equally endowed with the needs of consumption. In the *moshav* (*moshavim* in the Hebrew plural) each individual household maintains its own unit of production, with some measure of cooperation in marketing, while most of the services are cooperatively run. Until recently, these two types of Jewish agricultural settlement were tightly governed by rules of ownership and cooperation, and unlike the earlier *moshavot* were not prone to excessive growth and subsequent urbanization. Nevertheless, in spite of their small share in the Jewish population of Israel during the history of Jewish settlement in the country, the *kibbutzim* and *moshavim* commanded a high level of attention. They were pioneering social and economic forms that gained high priority from the Zionist organizations and were treated favorably by the socialist-oriented political parties. They were also often positively perceived by many as being in the forefront of the intensive process of Jewish settlement. The heyday of photographing the changing landscapes was in the early years of

Jewish statehood, starting with the establishment of the State of Israel on 14 May 1948. Hundreds of thousands of Jews, many of them arriving in the country as refugees, were on their way to settle in their new place of abode. The newly established state was suddenly filled with tents pitched in temporary camps, where

immigrants awaited permanent housing. These immigrant camps were usually set up on the outskirts of existing towns, or in areas zoned to become new towns or agricultural villages. Many of these new places were soon built up, with small houses spread over large areas. Early economic conditions were quite poor in these new immigrant settlements and housing was minimal in those days. Indeed, the houses seemed too small to accommodate the immigrant households that were sent to settle in them and perform the role of pioneers. The pictures of those days manage to vividly portray the emergency conditions of these early beginnings. These formative years of early statehood attracted photographers who were anxious to record yet another

phase of beginnings—the beginning of a new life in a new state. The establishment of new *moshavim* and towns for new immigrants in the Negev plains to the south or in the hilly regions of Galilee to the north, were recorded with a view to attest the form of the landscape at the outset. The thirty-odd new towns built in the country's periphery, to house the many immigrants and create a continuum of Jewish settlement so as to ensure a territorial hold in these regions, entailed a combination of pioneering heroism and social distress. The task was colored with geopolitical importance but the price was almost endemic poverty and unemployment.

The new towns were on the Israeli society's agenda for a long time and were impelled to wait patiently for some positive change in their economic fate. And then a process of change was set in motion. The small and modest houses that had been built on the barren landscape gave way to modern yet picturesque rural or urban landscapes. Even those immigrant settlers who came from undeveloped countries caught up with the pace of the country's change and development. Some of the once poor-looking immigrant settlements in the core of the country, especially *moshavim*, became comfortable suburban communities. The economic improvements brought about a complete transformation in some of the former immigrant towns, such as Yavne, south of Tel Aviv, and Rosh Ha'ayyin to the east. The central government supported the idea that wherever feasible it would encourage, through planning and subsidy, the attraction of a young middle-class population to these new towns. As a result, physical and social changes have taken place. The new immigrant towns of yesterday look very different today. Large residential quarters of semi-detached houses were added to these towns, providing a new architectural character. They no longer look like overextended public housing projects but contain components of middle-class residences. This kind of change, however, is not well documented by professional photographers. Some of the older and poorer sections of town are still waiting for change to come their way in the next decades, while others are already experiencing a move toward upgrading the existing housing.

Not only dedicated, professional photographers were documenting the changing landscape of the emerging State of Israel. Many of those who actually partook in the saga of early beginnings did so themselves and often with much joy. They were fulfilling their tasks with a strong sense of making history and believing that every step of their effort should be recorded. They wrote plenty of personal diaries and took the minutes of their public meetings in detail. They made sure that their achievements were documented by photographs. Therefore, we are able to follow their plight and joy and look at the changing landscape as it was experienced at each stage. Later on, when the changes were taken for granted, the minutes of meetings became brief and display no exciting spirit, while the photographs are mostly personal and set within the family. There is less sense of history in these later documents and the only way to revive it is by attempting to return to the few places that have been photographed with pride and care. The existing photographs can be compared with new pictures, the early views with the present ones, looking at the **then** and the **now**, and where possible and appropriate also adding the **in-between**. In this way we can appreciate the grand transformation that has taken place in Israel and how it has left its significant imprint on the landscape of the country.

Qiryat Gat is a fast growing city in 1997. New neighborhoods have been built in it in recent years to accommodate new immigrants from the former Soviet Union.

Jerusalem

In the middle of the nineteenth century, Jerusalem was a small town lying within its walls, its extent not much different from what it was in antiquity. The walls surrounding the Old City of Jerusalem were built in the sixteenth century, mostly along their line in the time of the Crusaders. The area between the Old City walls covers a little over a third of a square mile and at the beginning of the modern period, before the city began to spill beyond the walls, only about two thirds of the enclosed area was fully built up. There were large areas of open space, some of which were still under cultivation, supplying fruits and vegetables to the local residents, their numbers being quite small. In the early 1840s, a British Admiralty survey estimated the population of Jerusalem at only twelve thousand. The ancient shrines and the archeological sites of the Old City of Jerusalem stood regally for many centuries but the residential buildings, in which the contemporary population was living, as well as the alleys

and streets of the city, were in bad shape and full of squalor. Mark Twain, the famous American author, after visiting the city described the place in very uncomplimentary terms in his book of travels, *The Innocents Abroad*, published in 1869. This was, indeed, the bleak reality in the residential quarters of Jerusalem, a city enclosed within its walls, before the introduction of modern forms of urban development and the onset of new Jewish settlement. But this reality did not tarnish the charm of the city's landscape as seen from the surrounding mountains. Artists and later photographers were deeply taken by this charm and diligently and profusely documented the city as it was viewed from the distance. The walls of Jerusalem and the valleys that lie at their feet are the main features that stand out in these visual documents of a city just before it was to change its face.

A City Spreading Beyond Its Walls By the end of the nineteenth century the population of Jerusalem approached fifty thousand. By the end of the twentieth century, as a result of urban expansion in all directions — but mostly toward the west — the Old City itself was reduced to but a tiny section of a large metropolis with a population of over half a million, Jews and Arabs. Many of the residential areas of this metropolis are now quite far away from the Old City itself and are built on tops of mountains that not long ago were covered with rocks and shrubs. Over many decades since Twain's unhappy visit, the Old City walls witnessed a dynamic transformation of the surrounding landscape.

The gates of the Old City of Jerusalem saw many new kinds of people passing through them as visitors, traders or conquerors, all striving to share in the glory and spiritual significance of the city's past and in the promises that lay ahead. As more and more people traversed them, these gates became important sites of the city and many changes were made to improve access through them, to provide for commercial activities that tended to concentrate in their vicinities, inside and outside the walls, and to decorate them, thus adding to their attraction as architectural landmarks of the city. At the turn of the nineteenth century, the Ottoman rulers even added a tall clock tower over Jaffa Gate in the west of the Old City, to commemorate a quarter of a century of the contemporary sultan's rule, but the British, who came in their aftermath, were quick to dismantle it for aesthetic reasons, finding it too foreign and obtrusive. The anterior areas of each gate also underwent changes

over time, as the Old City increasingly became a focal point of tourism and commerce. Thus, the area outside Jaffa Gate (known in Arabic as the Al-Halil Gate, which refers to the ancient town of Hebron) became a focal site for commerce and transportation. So did the area in front of Damascus Gate (known in Hebrew as Shechem Gate, leading to Shechem, and in Arabic as

Jaffa Gate in the early twentieth century was a busy place.

Nablus Gate), facing north of Jerusalem. Stores clung to the walls of the Old City outside the gates and vendors' stands were spread all around. Horse-drawn carriages and donkeys were waiting outside the gates, offering their services to those who came and went, as can be seen in the photographs of those days. The British, who took it upon themselves to embellish the Old City, did away with all the structures that cluttered the entrances to the city and spoilt the architectural beauty of its walls and gates.

Many kinds of people came to take up residence in the city. The Western powers sent their consuls and other emissaries to increase their political hold in Jerusalem and the country at large, as well as to further their commercial interests in a region that had been pulled into modernization and economic development. Some of these new arrivals to the city built their residences in the open space outside the Old City, giving these areas a measure of prestige that later attracted other dignitaries and upwardly social mobile families to settle nearby. James Finn, the British consul in Jerusalem, and his wife Elizabeth, were among the well known foreign emissaries who built their homes on the outskirts of the Old City in the mid-nineteenth century. Finn even left detailed documentation in books later published in London of life in Jerusalem during that period. Another important role in the expansion beyond the city walls was played by the various Christian churches, especially those of European countries who were building new churches, monasteries, schools and other religious institutions in an effort to increase their presence in the holy city. Most of them could not find enough room to build spacious modern buildings in the midst of the congested Old City and therefore searched for sites outside the walls, although not too far away. One of the outstanding projects of this nature was the Russian Compound, built by the Russian Orthodox Church and the Czarist royal family. Besides church buildings with architectural features characteristic of the Russian Orthodox Church and of residential palaces for visiting nobility, the compound included huge dormitories for the many pilgrims who came each year from the Czarist Russian empire to pray at the religious sites of the city. The Russian Compound stood for many decades as the most prominent landmark on the high grounds northwest of the Old City walls, adjoining the main road leading from Jerusalem to the port city of Jaffa. The area surrounding the Russian Compound was uninhabited for some time and looked rural in character. Around it were but a few isolated houses. Today the Russian Compound stands in the middle of the commercial and administrative center of the modern city, a center densely built with an increasing number of tall

The Russian Compound in Jerusalem in the 1880s.

buildings. Likewise, areas in other directions around the Old City were only scattered with Arab villages, which looked very different from the new modern buildings springing up between them and the city walls. Most of the early buildings constructed outside the Old City were institutions or isolated homes. With time, however, entire residential neighborhoods joined them, gradually transforming the rural into an urban landscape. The new neighborhoods were intended to relieve residents of the crowded conditions within the Old City, where dwellings were scarce, and whatever was available was in very poor condition. The shortage of housing made rents exorbitant and certainly not affordable for the poorer tenants. The high density and the narrow alleys made it difficult to introduce the modern urban facilities that were now available thanks to the progress in modern science and technology. Moreover, the prevailing squalor deterred newcomers from settling within the city walls and as more new residents arrived in the city there was increasing interest in taking up the surrounding countryside for the development of newly planned residential neighborhoods. One of the earliest efforts to establish a residential hold outside the congested Old City was that of

Mishkenoth Sha'ananim, immediately to the west of the walls. It was a small housing project initiated in the late 1850s by Sir Moses Montefiore, a Jewish philanthropist-leader from Britain, who extended to Jerusalem the alms-house phenomenon that then existed in British cities, particularly in London, with the goal of serving the housing needs of the very poor. The project consisted of a series of terrace houses, containing over twenty small apartments as well as a flour windmill. Candidates for residence in the newly built Mishkenoth Sha'ananim neighborhood were not so easily found, however, despite the crowded conditions and high rents inside the city walls. They had to be lured by numerous financial incentives to come and stay in the newly constructed cottages at night. And they had good reason to be afraid. The new neighborhood could not provide what the city walls and their gates guaranteed: protection from robbers and other criminals who were harassing the countryside and made life there quite dangerous.

Although Mishkenoth Sha'ananim was a small neighborhood, it heralded a sizable development of Jewish neighborhoods that were to be established northwest of the Old City, some of them also originating in philanthropic initiatives, others built by local community leaders and even by business entrepreneurs. The reasons for this increased development were improved security conditions on the outskirts of the Old City and growing housing needs. More and more Jerusalemites, particularly Jews and Christians, moved out of the Old City. New residents arriving in the city also joined this process and settled in the new neighborhoods outside the Old City. All these construction efforts gradually transformed the open space outside the city walls into a mosaic of new neighborhoods, which eventually formed a city of its own with residential and commercial areas.

The Mahane Israel neighborhood west of the Old City of Jerusalem in the late nineteenth century.

The Old City gradually deteriorated into one of the less desirable residential parts of the city as the more modern, affluent elements left it for the new areas. The Jewish population of Jerusalem was particularly active in building its own new neighborhoods, mainly in the northwestern sector, not far from the main road to the coastal plain—the Jaffa road. Immediately west of the Old City, on the road leading southwest from Jaffa gate, stands another one of Jerusalem's first Jewish neighborhoods, Mahane Israel. Initiated by a local group, it was founded in the late 1860s. The founders were Jews from Morocco, known then as the Ma'araviyyim or Mughrabim ("Westerners"). Headed by their rabbi, this Jewish group wanted to establish its own ethnic hold in a separate neighborhood outside the crowded Old City. For many decades Mahane Israel did not grow and remained small. Like most of the other new Jewish neighborhoods being built to the northwest of Jerusalem, it was only many decades later that the vicinity of Mahane Israel was modernized. Modern residential homes, commercial buildings and institutions were established, including the Jerusalem YMCA compound and the prestigious King David Hotel. Toward the end of the twentieth century, the area next to Mahane Israel, known as Mamilla (literally "water from God," because of the large water pond lying nearby), was also undergoing substantial urban redevelopment.

Almost concomitantly with Mahane Israel, the Jewish neighborhood of Nahalat Shiv'a was established on Jaffa Road in 1869. This was founded by a group of Ashkenazi and Sephardic Jews who were distressed by the crowded conditions and exorbitant rents in the Old City. Nahalat Shiv'a was built not far from the Russian Compound, and at first many of the Jews living in the Old City doubted its security — without the protection of walls and gates. Nevertheless, the location of Nahalat Shiv'a on Jaffa Road, which in later years became the main commercial artery of modern Jerusalem, brought a wealth of urban development to the neighborhood's surroundings. Gradually, commercial and office

buildings rose along Jaffa Road, dwarfing the old neighborhood and threatening its existence, as this also raised the value of real estate in the area. But the municipality of Jerusalem and its city planners quickly realized the potential value of preserving Nahalat Shiv'a in its old form and were instrumental in turning the neighborhood into a cluster of art studios, restaurants and tourist oriented stores. Nahalat Shiv'a is no longer a residential area, yet it has maintained the old atmosphere of its early beginnings in its narrow alleys and architectural style.

Top: The Nahalat Shiv'a neighborhood along Jaffa Road in Jerusalem in 1910.

Bottom: The Sha'arei Zedeq hospital on Jaffa Road in Jerusalem at the turn of the twentieth century.

Another of the earlier Jewish neighborhoods is Me'a She'arim, which was built in the 1870s by a large group of Jewish families—over one hundred of them living in the Old City—who joined together to form a company for the purpose of erecting an entire neighborhood in accordance with some modern principles of urban planning but also following the requirements of the religiously orthodox Jewish way of life. In its early days, Me'a She'arim was an innovative combination of modernity in the physical sense and tradition in the cultural sense. It represented a bold attempt on the part of Old City dwellers to improve their housing conditions without dispensing with their old ways. In the long run, they were successful: not only has the neighborhood remained a strictly religious community all these years, but has also served as an initiative for the development of a series of new neighborhoods in the vicinity, all following this blend of physical modernity and religious orthodoxy. Thus, a stretch of religiously orthodox and even ultra-orthodox neighborhoods now reach westward from Me'a She'arim, the mother of them all, to the western edge of the city.

Some Christian groups, coming from abroad, also made an effort to strike root in the newly built areas outside the Old City and developed their own neighborhoods. One such neighborhood, known as the German Colony, was established in 1873 by the Temple Society (*Tempelgesellschaft*), a unique Christian community originating in southern Germany, whose goal was to rebuild the Holy Land as a Christian country and for this purpose established several other such colonies around the country, including two near Jaffa and one near Haifa. The

The German Colony in Jerusalem in the late nineteenth century.

German Colony in Jerusalem was initially built along a main street in the style of a *strassendorf* (street village), a design particularly common in its country of origin. It brought to the outskirts of Jerusalem a taste of a comparatively modern style of residence with its spacious detached houses, lined up in a pre-planned setting. A hundred years later, the houses of this neighborhood, still known as the German Colony by Jerusalemites although the former German residents are long gone elsewhere, are sought by middle-class families as romantic and comfortable residences. Next to the old homes new residential buildings have been added to the neighborhood, some of them trying to maintain the character of the old ones.

The development of the German Colony has signaled the way for other such neighborhoods outside the Old City walls. Not far from the German Colony, some wealthy Christian Arab families also chose to build their new homes outside the Old City walls. They established a circle of such neighborhoods in the southwestern sector of the new part of the city, Qatamon and Baq'a being the more prominent of these communities. For a long time, they provided an elegant and quasi-suburban environment for the middle-class population of Christian Arabs and Europeans. As such, when the British arrived to rule the country and partake in its economic development, these Arab neighborhoods constituted convenient locations in which they could reside. The Muslim population of the Old City was less engaged in moving beyond the walls as the Christians and Jews were doing. It was poorer and more dependent on the cheap rental housing provided by the Muslim religious trust, the *Waqf*. It was mainly the more affluent Muslim families that built new neighborhoods not far from the Old City. These were largely clusters of houses of members of the same clan or *hamuleh*. The Nashashibi clan initiated the development of the Sheikh Jarrah neighborhood on the north side of the Old City, near the Nablus road. In the same northerly direction the Hussaini clan had founded neighborhoods of its own. With time, these Muslim neighborhoods as well as others, north of the Old City walls, became the commercial and business center of the Arab population in Jerusalem, especially since 1948, when Jerusalem was divided between Israel and Jordan. The older Nablus road and the newer Salah a-Din street now constitute the main axes of the urban center that serves the Palestinian-Arab population in the eastern part of the city.

Garden Neighborhoods The Jewish middle-class population of Jerusalem continued its search for areas in which to develop its own new neighborhoods. The great move in this direction started in the 1920s under the British. One of the opportunities for achieving this goal occurred when the Greek Orthodox Church, a primary landowner in the surroundings of Jerusalem, became hard pressed for financial resources. Prior to 1917, the Russian czar had been a major source of funding for this church, but as a result of the Russian defeat in the Russo-Japanese War in 1905, funds were cut short creating a serious financial crisis in the Jerusalem-based church. The crisis was deepened with the demise of the Czarist regime following revolution and all funds were totally cut. Pressured by the new British administration in the country, the Greek Orthodox Church in Jerusalem had to sell some of its land for urban development. This large sale of land had a substantial impact on the growth of the city. Many prestigious neighborhoods and public buildings of modern Jerusalem owe their beginnings to this dramatic event in the city's real estate market. Several areas were purchased by a land development company of the Zionist Organization, one of which was allocated for the construction of a neighborhood named Rehavia. It was built close to the center of the new city, on a hill overlooking the Monastery of the Cross, an important site in the early history of Christianity. Early in the twentieth century, the area was still devoid of buildings, except for a windmill for wheat grinding. Today the windmill is hidden between a large hotel building and a small shopping center. Plans for the Rehavia neighborhood were drawn in line with the "garden city" concept, by Richard Kaufman,

Above: Ben-Maimon Boulevard in the Rehavia neighborhood of Jerusalem in the 1930s.

Below: The first bus in Jerusalem's Talpiyyot neighborhood in the early 1920s.

one of the influential Jewish architects of the time, who made a remarkable impact on the landscape transformation in the country. This new neighborhood, along with some others around the city, was built along the lines that had emerged in previous decades in Britain under the garden city movement. The guiding concept of these plans was to provide a pleasant residential environment with a large proportion of gardens and other kinds of open space on the periphery of cities. This concept underlined the construction of some of the new Jewish neighborhoods on the northern edge of Jaffa and on the slopes of Mount Carmel in Haifa. In Jerusalem itself two additional Jewish neighborhoods — Talpiyyot and Bet Hakerem — were built along the lines of the "garden city" concept. But while this concept was guiding the early construction of Rehavia, it soon became obvious that the Jewish elite was drawn to it and interested in finding a place of residence there. Very soon, what had been visualized as a quasi-suburban neighborhood of detached homes had become a fully-fledged urban neighborhood of middle-rise residential buildings. As the demand for a place in Rehavia increased, the buildings rose even higher, and a cluster of high-rise towers named the Wolfson Towers, was eventually built nearby. In the 1920s, those who could not afford the high prices of land were impelled to move much further into the city's periphery to achieve the goal of garden neighborhood living. One group of lower middle-class families— teachers, clerks and authors—established the neighborhood of Bet Hakerem in the far western end of the city, at the time beyond the city limits. Another such group went to the southernmost edge of the city to establish the garden neighborhood of Talpiyyot. Bet Hakerem, like Rehavia, has now lost most of its detached homes and has turned into a fully-fledged urban section of town. Talpiyyot had to wait much longer. Already in the early 1920s, it became clear that because this new community, in the far south of the city, lay isolated from other Jewish neighborhoods and was cut off by a belt of Arab residential areas, it was much less desirable and considered less safe than other alternatives. Its development lagged behind for years, especially between 1948 and 1967, when Talpiyyot stood on the borders of a city divided between Israel and Jordan. It was only after the Six-Day War in

June 1967 that Talpiyyot was awakened from its dormancy in the corner of the city and became the focus of increased residential construction. The old garden neighborhood disappeared and in its place urban styled residential buildings now dominate Talpiyyot and its surroundings. Only a few of the original homes survived.

The 1920s also witnessed the establishment of the Hebrew University on Mount Scopus, northeast of the Old City. As a result, the city gradually developed into a major center of learning for the Jewish population, even attracting students from abroad. The university added a Jewish landmark to the mountainous skyline to the east of the Old City, joining the tower of the Russian Church on the Mount of Olives, the nearby mosque minaret of the rural Arab suburb of At-Tur on the crest of the Mount of Olives and the tower of Augusta Victoria, a large building constructed by the German Kaiser Wilhelm II on the occasion of his visit to Jerusalem in 1898.

The garden neighborhoods of Jerusalem, though they have much engaged the writers of the history and the geography of the city, took up only a small portion of the Jewish construction in the new city during the years of the British period. Most of this construction took place in the more central parts of the city, starting on both sides of Jaffa Road and then along King George V Street. The latter was festively inaugurated in 1925 and since then tall buildings have risen near it as well as along Ben-Yehuda Street which it intersected. The center of the new city, now marked by the triangle of the three aforementioned streets, was transformed during the 1920s and 1930s from an assemblage of a few scattered houses into a large concentration of urban-looking buildings that would fit, in those years, the centers of many cities in Europe. As time went by high-rise buildings were added to the center and the landscape transformation continued, to the dismay of those trying to preserve its architectural character as it took shape by the middle of the twentieth century.

A Divided City In 1948, the British left the country and in the aftermath of the war waged between Arabs and Jews that year, the city of Jerusalem was divided between Israel and Jordan. The western part of the city was held by Israel, the eastern part by Jordan. The Hebrew University campus remained an Israeli enclave surrounded by Jordanian-held territory. Each side developed its own sector in different ways. Israel made Jerusalem its capital and devoted many resources to urban development, mainly to the west, toward the corridor connecting the Israeli part of the city to the rest of the new state. The Jordanians kept the city of Amman, east of the Jordan river, as their capital, while holding Jerusalem secondary in terms of development priorities. The Israeli side of the city experienced substantial changes after 1948. The Knesset (the Israeli parliament) was set up in the city, first downtown and later on a hill to the west of the city center. New Jewish immigrants settled in old as well as new neighborhoods built on the immediate outskirts. The Hebrew University campus was reestablished not far from the Knesset building, leaving behind the inaccessible old campus on

The new Knesset building in Jerusalem in the late 1960s.

Mount Scopus. Population growth and economic development brought about the construction of high-rise buildings — offices, hotels and residences — in the central areas of the city. This process gained momentum through time, eventually changing the skyline of the western part of the city. Jerusalem gradually lost its old image and grew more and more like a modern metropolis.

A Reunited Growing City Another dramatic change took place in the city as a result of the 1967 War, which ended in Israel's taking control of the entire region of Jerusalem. Subsequently, the Israeli government encouraged the construction of new Jewish neighborhoods on the outskirts of the city, all under one municipality. On the southern edge of the city, on a mountain ridge overlooking the city toward the north and Bethlehem toward the south, new Jewish neighborhoods were built in the Gilo quarter. In the southeastern corner, next to the former residence of the British High Commissioner, the neighborhood of Eastern Talpiyyot was built. In the extended northern sections of the city a long series of Jewish quarters and neighborhoods have been added since 1967: Ramot Eshkol, Giv'at Shapira ("French Hill"), Pisgat Ze'ev, Neve Ya'aqov and Ramot Allon. Parts of the Pisgat Ze'ev neighborhood were still under construction in the late 1990s, when a new neighborhood of Haredi (ultra-orthodox) Jewish residents was added to its periphery. As a result of this massive construction, the mountains around Jerusalem, for many years part of the countryside surrounding the city, were gradually covered with extensively built-up areas and streets, changing the skyline once again. These were three decades of dramatic urban change, the like of which the city had never witnessed before in terms of the scale and expanse of residential construction in all directions.

Settlements on the Way to the City Development in areas adjacent to Jerusalem have echoed those taking place within the city. Jewish settlements have been established around the city in several directions, but the first thrust toward this progress transpired to the west of Jerusalem — in the mountainous area along the main highways linking Jerusalem and the coastal plain, particularly along the Jerusalem–Tel Aviv road. In the early 1890s, the small *moshava* of Moza was established by the side of this road by a group of Jewish Jerusalemites. It has remained very small over the years,

The beginnings of Kibbutz Qiryat Anavim in the mountains west of Jerusalem in the early 1920s.

never growing to become a sizable place. In the same decade as Moza was built, another *moshava* named Har Tuv was established in the hills west of the Jerusalem mountains. It too did not enjoy growth and prosperity and eventually ceased to exist in 1948 as a result of the hostilities between Arabs and Jews. Altogether, during the late Ottoman period there was very little Jewish settlement in the mountains west of Jerusalem. Most of the effort of Jewish residential construction was concentrated within the city and its immediate outskirts. Even during the British period, only very few Jewish settlements were built in the mountains to the west of the city of Jerusalem. At that time most of the settlements in the region were Arab. Two *kibbutzim* were established during this period, the first one, Qiryat Anavim, was founded in the early 1920s on Jewish owned land, originally planned to be developed as a residential suburb of Jerusalem, a plan which did not materialize. In the 1930s, another attempt to develop a Jewish residential suburb nearby failed and in its place a *kibbutz* named Ma'ale Hahamisha was founded, adjacent to the Arab village of Abu-Ghosh. These two *kibbutzim* tried hard to develop a mountain agriculture, not well known until then among Jewish settlers in the country. Eventually, a resort industry, based on the cool summer and the fine landscape of the mountain environment, provided a viable economic base for the two early settlements as well as others that followed them in later years. The main road running between Jerusalem and the coastal plain was gradually improved. It ceased to be a stony carriage road and was turned into an asphalt-covered highway, easing access not only to Jerusalem but also to the settlements on the way, rendering them more accessible for tourists and vacationers.

After Israel was founded as a state in 1948, the open areas included within Jerusalem's western boundaries and known as the Jerusalem Corridor were settled by a large number of new Jewish settlements. Most of them were immigrant *moshavim* that replaced the Arab villages existing there before 1948. They started with agriculture as

their main livelihood, horticulture being the main endeavor. But the mountainous soils were rather poor and the terrace cultivation not suitable for modern agriculture and a considerable number of the new villagers turned to the city for work. Many of the *moshavim* in the Jerusalem mountains gradually became commuting rural suburbs. The small farm houses changed into spacious villas, some built by urbanites moving into the adjacent countryside in order to realize their dream of "a house and a garden." This kind of change took place first in *moshavim* close to Jerusalem but later spread further west, beyond the edge of the mountains. The two Arab villages that remained in the Jerusalem mountains, Abu-Ghosh and Ein Rafa, followed the path of the Jewish *moshavim*

and gradually grew as rural suburbs of Jerusalem. Agriculture ceased to be their main source of livelihood. Abu-Ghosh sits near the highway and has turned into a cluster of road services, famous for its Oriental-style restaurants. The villages have grown in size and expanded into former fields and gardens. Yesterday they were small and compact settlements stuck at the top of the slope, but today they are spread out all over it down to the bottom of the valley. In recent decades, the Jerusalem Corridor has become increasingly suburbanized as more of the city's residents have opted to move there. A striking instance is in Mevasseret Ziyyon, once two adjoining immigrant settlements established in the early 1950s on either side of the Jerusalem–Tel Aviv highway. For years these places were never noticed by the urban middle class. But as the government agencies moved to develop new residential areas by making it possible to build new spacious residences there, many Jerusalemites opted to move there, commuting daily to the city. Within only two decades, Mevasseret Ziyyon grew to become a sizable town just west of Jerusalem. New neighborhoods have sprung all over the mountain crest and now herald to the traveler coming from the west the arrival into the Jerusalem metropolis.

Top: Moshav Giv'at Ye'arim in the mountains west of Jerusalem was established by new immigrants from Yemen in the early 1950s.

Bottom: Kibbutz Zor'a in the foothills west of Jerusalem in its early beginnings in 1949. It was established primarily by immigrants from South Africa.

The road to Jerusalem at the entrance to the Jerusalem mountains (Sha'ar Hagay in Hebrew and Bab al-Wad in Arabic) in the late nineteenth century. Transportation was by horse-drawn carriages, stopping to rest at the khan (hostel) on the right side of the road.

Another immigrant town that was established in the 1950s far west of Jerusalem is Bet Shemesh. For years the town was outside the main course of development. Its housing was largely of the types common within the public housing sector: large and unattractive apartment buildings. However, in the 1970s an effort was made to build residential settings of a better quality with the hope of attracting to the town new residents of a relatively higher social status. But the more substantial transformation of Bet Shemesh started to take place in the mid-1990s. Following the large influx into the country of immigrants from countries of the former Soviet Union, the central government made an effort to open up new housing opportunities in many places around the country, but especially in more peripheral towns. Bet Shemesh was chosen to harbor much of this new development and is now undergoing considerable change as a result. New neighborhoods have been built and others are being planned to be built in the near future. Hills that just yesterday consisted of large expanses of open space covered with natural vegetation are being built over. There are those who hail it as progress; others lament the damage done to nature. Either way, the former landscape is being transformed in Bet Shemesh as it has been in other parts of the Jerusalem periphery.

The development of Jerusalem into a large modern city and the transformation of the Jerusalem Corridor into a suburban strip beyond it is reflected in the changing highway running between Jerusalem and the coastal plain. Once a narrow and winding stony road, the highway is now laid with two asphalt lanes for each direction, allowing a swift flow of traffic. There is no longer any need for the services of the *khan*—the roadside

The khan at Sha'ar Hagay is now defunct. Fast automobiles, using a greatly improved highway, have no need to rest, as carriages had to in the old days.

hostel — at the entrance to the Jerusalem mountains. The *khan* has been left standing there, and for years deserted. It has served to remind the hurried car riders of the old days — when the journey from Old Jaffa to Old Jerusalem took more than a day instead of today's hour, and when the country's landscape was starkly different from what it is today.

A few miles east of Jerusalem is located the new town of Ma'ale Adumim. It was established in the mid-1970s when Israelis began to settle in newly founded Jewish settlements near Jerusalem beyond the 'Green Line' that separated Israel from Jordanian-held territories between 1949 and 1967. Ma'ale Adumim was built in a mountainous terrain marked by desert conditions. It stands out in the landscape of the Judean desert which for many centuries has known only encampments of nomads, hideouts of the religiously devout or some military strongholds. Following Ma'ale Adumim, other new Jewish settlements have been built north and south of the city, beyond the 'Green Line.' They are part of the growing and expanding suburbs of the city of Jerusalem. All around the city there is intensive construction of housing, mostly for Jews but also by Palestinians, who constitute a sizable portion of the population in the eastern half of the metropolitan region. Green open space is giving way to suburban development in the western part of the region. Barren hills are being covered by housing in the eastern part of the Jerusalem metropolis, well within the Judean Desert.

A view of the Old City of Jerusalem in the early twentieth century. On its eastern side stands the Dome of the Rock, a Muslim shrine, flanked by the Western Wall. The Jewish Quarter is in the foreground with its two large domed synagogues.

Opposite: The Jewish Quarter was badly damaged in 1948 during the War of Independence when the Jewish inhabitants were forced to leave it for the western side of the city. After 1967 substantial rehabilitation took place in the Jewish Quarter.

Left: A view of the area adjacent to the Western Wall at the end of the twentieth century (1997). A large plaza was built in front of the Western Wall to serve the many visitors and pilgrims who frequent it. The Hebrew University campus is seen on Mount Scopus on the far skyline, behind the Dome of the Rock.

Below: In the early twentieth century the area adjacent to the Western Wall, near the Jewish Quarter, was occupied by the small Mughrabi neighborhood, built in the middle of the nineteenth century. The far background is dominated by Mount Scopus, still without buildings or trees. In the far left is the Augusta Victoria compound built by the German Emperor Wilhelm II.

Top: Beduin tents outside Damascus Gate in the middle of the
nineteenth century.

Right: Shops leaning against the walls at Damascus Gate at the turn of the
twentieth century.

Left: Taxi cabs standing by Damascus Gate in the 1930s.

Opposite: Damascus Gate at the end of the twentieth century.

Top: Before the First World War the Ottoman authorities, celebrating the long reign of their sultan, erected a clock tower over the Jaffa Gate.

Center: On 11 December 1917 General Allenby marched with his mounted British troops to celebrate his capture of the city of Jerusalem from the Ottomans. Jaffa Road near Jaffa Gate was fully built at the time, with stores, offices and hotels lining both sides. The buildings on the right lean on the Old City wall.

Bottom: General Allenby as he walks into the Old City after passing through Jaffa Gate. As he approached Jaffa Gate, General Allenby dismounted his horse to prepare himself to enter the Old City on foot, as a sign of respect to Jerusalem and its history.

Opposite: The area outside Jaffa Gate looks very different nowadays from what it was in the early years of the twentieth century. Immediately after the First World War the British authorities removed the clock tower from the top of the gate, as well as various structures that leaned on the city walls near the gate. After the 1967 Six-Day War the Israeli authorities began a series of projects that changed the entrance for automobiles to the Old City through Jaffa Gate.

Left: In the 1880s, Jaffa Road just outside Jaffa Gate already had a row of stores on each side. The street itself was not yet fully paved. Donkeys and horse-drawn carriages were still the only means of transportation.

Top: Jaffa Road in the early 1920s. Carriages and animals were still the main means of transportation. The Ottoman clock tower has been transferred from the top of Jaffa Gate to the plaza in front of it.

Center: Jaffa Road near Jaffa Gate in the early 1930s. Buses and cars have taken over from the carriages. A traffic policeman was a new addition to the modernizing urban landscape. The Ottoman clock tower has been transferred to a new location.

Bottom: At the end of the twentieth century, Jaffa Road near the Jaffa Gate looks very different. The walls of the Old City are now fully exposed. The commercial center that once existed next to the wall disappeared and was replaced by an open park.

Right: The Tower of David – a view of the citadel from outside Jaffa Gate in a photograph taken in the 1880s. The citadel has ancient foundations. During the Ottoman period it served as a military garrison. The area outside Jaffa Gate functioned as a market.

Bottom: The Tower of David – a view of the citadel from outside Jaffa Gate in 1934. By now taxis and buses have taken over from the carriages. The British authorities opened a museum of Jerusalem ethnography in the citadel – displaying mostly traditional costumes – and thus transforming the age-old military function of the place.

Top: The Tower of David – a view of the citadel in 1997. Though the tower remained as it had been over many ages, its surroundings beyond the wall have undergone continuous change since 1967. The structure in the foreground is a huge underground parking area for the many visitors who enter the Old City via Jaffa Gate. The citadel now houses a museum of the city's history.

*Opposite: A view from the southwest of the Russian Compound in the 1860s.
The compound, built between 1857 and 1860 northwest of the Old City, comprised a
church and hostels for the many Russian pilgrims. The Old City is to the right. The
future Jaffa Road, the main street of the new city, will eventually run along the dirt road
marked by a stone fence immediately to the right of the Russian Compound. The plowed
field in the center of the photograph is where, in the 1870s, the Jewish neighborhood
Nahalat Shiv'a was to be built.*

*Top: The Russian Compound, its former hostel buildings now serving as the site of the
Jerusalem District Court and other such official functions, stands in the middle of
Jerusalem's center . Close by, to the left, is the new city hall. Jaffa Road runs from left to
right. On the road to the right is a high-rise office building that stands on the edge of the
Nahalat Shiv'a neighborhood. In the middle on the far horizon is the campus of the
Hebrew University on Mount Scopus.*

Mishkenoth Sha'ananim, the first Jewish neighborhood built outside the city walls, was initiated by Sir Moses Montefiore in the late 1850s. The windmill was part of the project. Very few houses stood outside the walls at that time.

*Top: In the 1880s Mishkenoth Sha'ananim was joined by another Jewish neighborhood –
Yemin Moshe – named after Sir Moses Montefiore. The new neighborhood is on the right of the photograph.
Following the 1948 war, when the city was divided between Israel and Jordan, the two neighborhoods found
themselves on a hostile frontier. For several decades after the war, they deteriorated and were inhabited by
poor families.*

*Bottom: Today Mishkenoth Sha'ananim houses a hotel and a music center, and Yemin Moshe has
transformed into a prestigious neighborhood.*
*The poor families were relocated to other parts of the city, and others, who had the economic means to
rehabilitate and renovate, were invited to settle in the neighborhood. In the meantime, tall hotel buildings
were constructed behind the two neighborhoods, changing the visual image that had characterized the city in
the early years of its expansion beyond the city walls.*

Top: Much of the early urban development outside the Old City walls took place on the west side, along Jaffa Road (on the left of the photograph) and Mamilla Street (on the right). In the center is the Mamilla Pond, situated in the middle of a Muslim cemetery. On the other side of Mamilla Street lies Mahane Israel, one of the earliest Jewish neighborhood outside the Old City. It was built in 1868 by Jews from North Africa, mostly from Morocco.

Bottom: A view of the built-up area immediately west of the Old City in 1938.

Opposite: Nowadays Mamilla Pond and the cemetery consist of a large open urban space in the heart of Jerusalem. It is joined by Independence Park, cultivated as a green area in the middle of the city.

A view of the Mount of Olives in the 1880s. Near the Jericho Road lies the old Jewish cemetery. Several churches, including the Russian Church of Mary Magdalen distinguished by its onion-shaped domes, were built on the lower slope of the mountain, close to the Garden of Getsemene, where Jesus and his disciples retired to meditate and pray, and where Jesus spent the last night before his arrest.

Above: Jewish burial on the Mount of Olives (on the right) was interrupted in 1948, as a result of the division of the city between Israel and Jordan. The Jordanians built a hotel on top of the mountain. After the 1967 Six-Day War, Jewish burial was resumed, and large parts of the cemetery were repaired.

Left: The Church of All Nations was built on the lower slope of the Mount of Olives in the years 1919-1924. Many Catholic nations joined in funding the construction of this church, hence its name.

Left: A view of the Russian Compound from the north in a photograph taken in the 1880s. The buildings in the foreground are situated along what would later evolve as the Street of the Prophets. The large building on the skyline to the far left is the yet incomplete Ethiopian Church. In the 1890s a dome was added to the church.

Top: Today the Church of the Russian Compound is integrated in the busiest section of the city. The formerly empty areas are now fully built up.

Center: A view photographed in 1937 of the area immediately east of the northern wall of the Old City. On the left skyline is the French Catholic hostel Notre Dame de France. In the center is the Ethiopian Church. The road in the foreground, running north from Herod Gate, eventually emerged as the Salah a-Din Street, the main commercial street of East Jerusalem.

Bottom: Salah a-Din Street in East Jerusalem in 1997.

Top: Me'a She'arim was one of the first Jewish neighborhoods in Jerusalem to be built outside the Old City to the northwest of Damascus Gate. In the mid-1890s the neighborhood was still quite isolated.

Bottom: Hewing stones in 1925 for the construction of new homes in the vicinity of Batei Ungarn, a new Jewish neighborhood built next to Me'a She'arim.

Opposite: Nowadays Me'a She'arim is an old neighborhood surrounded by newer ones. The old neighborhood can easily be distinguished by its tiled roofs.

Above: A view of the nascent campus of the Hebrew University on Mount Scopus in a photograph taken in the early 1930s from the north-eastern corner of the Old City walls. What was then the library building stands prominent against the skyline. Additional buildings were constructed in ensuing decades. Between 1948 and 1967, when Jerusalem was divided between Israel and Jordan, Mount Scopus remained an Israeli enclave within Jordanian territory, and the Hebrew University operated in the western part of the city.

Right: After 1967, since the unification of Jerusalem in the Six-Day War, a large campus for the Hebrew University was rebuilt on top of Mount Scopus, as seen in the picture taken in 1997.

Above: A view of the Old City of Jerusalem from Mount Scopus, in a photograph taken in the 1880s. The northeastern areas outside the walls are almost empty of buildings. In the foreground are olive trees scattered in the valley.

Left: A view of the Old City from Mount Scopus taken in 1997. Much of the northwestern areas outside the Old City are covered with Arab neighborhoods built in recent decades. In the 1930s the Rockefeller Museum was built near the northeastern corner of the Old City, outside the walls.

Top: The Alliance Israelite vocational school building on Jaffa Street, towards the end of the nineteenth century. The school was opened in 1882 by the Alliance Israelite Society of Paris, to foster vocational training for Jewish boys in Jerusalem.

Center: A class at the Alliance Israelite school towards the end of the nineteenth century. Note the fez hats typical to those years, when the country was still under Ottoman rule.

Bottom: In the 1990s the site of the former Alliance Israelite vocational school on Jaffa Road was taken over by a large and tall commercial building named Merkaz Clal. The old school building was demolished in 1970.

Opposite: The Merkaz Clal building shadows over Jaffa Road, the main commercial street in the center of Jerusalem. To the upper right are the old Jewish neighborhoods of Mazkeret Moshe and Ohel Moshe, built in the 1880s and still preserving their old architectural style.

52

Top: King George V Street was opened in 1925 in a festive ceremony. In the late 1920s there were only a few buildings along it. In the background is the Ratisbonne French Catholic monastery, the construction of which was completed in the mid 1890s. Gradually new residential and commercial buildings were added along the street, and since the middle of the 1930s it has been one of the main commercial and institutional thoroughfares of the city.

Bottom: In 1997 King George V Street is sided by tall buildings, most of them for commercial use.

*Top: Facing north toward Jaffa Road from the intersection of King George V,
Mamilla and Ramban streets in the late 1920s. Ramban Street on the left is still unpaved,
it did not have sidewalks yet, and people walked in the middle of the street.
There is only little automobile traffic. In the far distance are the buildings of the Bezalel
Art School, situated in a street parallel to King George V Street.*

*Bottom: Tall buildings, including two hotels, are rising on both sides of King George V
Street, at its intersection with Ramban and Agron (formerly Mamilla) Streets.
Nowadays King George V Street is a major traffic artery connecting the city center
with the southern neighborhoods.*

Top: In 1924, Ben-Yehuda Street, now in the commercial center of Jerusalem, was still a residential street lined with only a few family homes. An early commercial building (notice the commercial signs above the entrances) was constructed further up the street. The photograph was taken from the intersection of Ben-Yehuda Street with Jaffa Road, known as Zion Square (Kikar Ziyyon in Hebrew).

Center: Ben-Yehuda Street in 1930 was a fully-fledged urban street. Taxicabs are waiting in line for passengers in the middle of the street.

Bottom: Ben-Yehuda Street in 1944. A British military truck is seen in Zion Square.

Opposite: Part of Ben-Yehuda Street is now a pedestrian mall. Further along the street, at its intersection with King George V Street, a tall office building towers over the city center.

Above: Rehavia, the first Jewish garden neighborhood to be built in Jerusalem, is located on a hill overlooking the Monastery of the Cross, within walking distance of King George V Street. In this photograph, dated to the 1900s, the hill has no buildings on it, except for a windmill that operated in the empty area. Construction started in Rehavia in the early 1920s.

Opposite: Rehavia nowadays is a long established residential neighborhood. Most of the original single-family houses have given way to apartment buildings of three to seven floors. The trees planted in this garden neighborhood in the 1920s and 1930s are now tall enough to match the buildings next to them.

Top: Since the 1880s, a series of Jewish neighborhoods was built along Jaffa Road, close to the commercial center and the Mahane Yehuda market. These neighborhoods, nowadays known collectively as Nahla'ot, are inhabited by a variety of Jewish ethnic groups. The photograph was taken in the early 1960s.

Bottom: The Nahla'ot area has recently been undergoing a process of gentrification. Old houses are being renovated, and new ones are being built. On the skyline beyond these neighborhoods, one can see tall buildings rising in the nearby downtown.

Top: The neighborhood of Rehavia and the adjoining Sha'arei Hesed neighborhood to its left in a view from the early 1960s. Sha'arei Hesed is one of the Jewish neighborhoods built just before the First World War in the old architectural style of the late Ottoman era.

Bottom: Sha'arei Hesed now hides behind the Wolfson Towers complex of high-rise residential buildings, constructed on the adjoining slope. The Wolfson Towers are a far cry from the cozy atmosphere still found in the old houses of nearby Sha'arei Hesed.

Right: The Arab village of Ein Karim in the 1880s was situated several miles outside the city of Jerusalem. Ein Karim is identified as the biblical City of Judah, the birthplace of John the Baptist, and the village visited by Mary. It harbors several Christian churches and a monastery.

Below: En Kerem, as it is called in Hebrew, is now a suburban neighborhood on the western edge of Jerusalem. It has become increasingly attractive to those who value its picturesque setting, and new houses have been added. The formerly bare mountains beyond En Kerem have been planted with trees, now the Jerusalem Forest.

Below: In 1935 the road between Tel Aviv and Jerusalem wound down the bare slope near the Jewish village of Moza in seven bends, known as the "Seven Sisters".

Opposite: The barren mountains next to the Tel Aviv-Jerusalem road have by now been built up with the residential town of Mevasseret Ziyyon or planted with pines. Near the old winding road now stands a home for the aged.

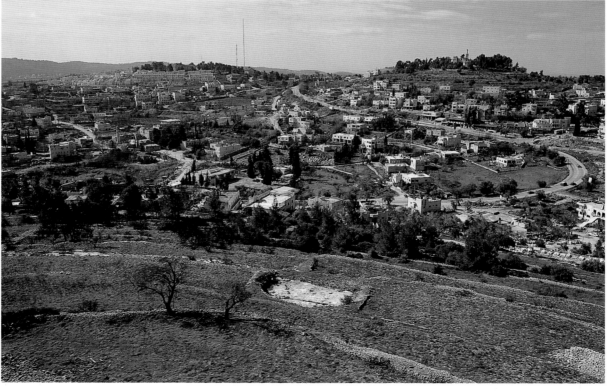

Above: The Arab village of Abu-Ghosh in the Jerusalem mountains, west of the city, in 1938. The village clusters on a hill to the left of the then main road to Jerusalem from the coast.

Right: The Arab village of Abu-Ghosh in 1997 is spread over a much larger area than six decades earlier. The main road to Jerusalem was moved beyond the hill and the Jewish town of Qiryat Ye'arim was added on the skyline behind Abu-Ghosh.

Above: Kibbutz Qiryat Anavim in the Jerusalem mountains, west of the city, in 1938. Orchard-growing was an important component in the economy of this mountain kibbutz. The member of the Jewish Settlement Police sitting on guard on the right side of the picture, signifies the times – the Arab uprising in the country during 1936-1939.

Left: Kibbutz Qiryat Anavim six decades later, leans heavily on tourism and resort activities for its livelihood, as do nowadays other kibbutzim and moshavim in the Jerusalem mountains.

Bet Shemesh as viewed from the northeast, in a photograph taken in 1952. The newly established town is one of a series of such new towns built in the country's periphery, and housing newly arrived immigrants. Some of the inhabitants of Bet Shemesh still live in temporary huts made of corrugated iron, seen in the center of the photograph.

Bet Shemesh at the end of the 1990s is a much larger town than it had been in the 1950s. The top of the hill is now covered with tall apartment buildings. Further to the south new neighborhoods have been added and others are being planned, so that eventually Bet Shemesh will become a large city of more than a hundred thousand inhabitants.

Right: An aerial view of Bet Shemesh in 1997 reveals a small town in the process of becoming a large city.

Tel Aviv-Yafo

The official name of the city of Tel Aviv is now Tel Aviv-Yafo, which is how it appears on current maps. Although its municipality also carries this name, most people still refer to it as Tel Aviv. The name Tel Aviv-Yafo points to the historical fact that until 1948, there had been two adjacent towns—almost unwilling twins—one an Arab town called Jaffa and the other a Jewish town called Tel Aviv. At the turn of the twentieth century,

only Jaffa functioned as a city, home to an overwhelming Arab majority and a Jewish minority. Gradually, as Jewish immigration into the country accelerated toward the end of the nineteenth century, some Jewish neighborhoods were founded on the northern outskirts of Jaffa, Neve Zedeq

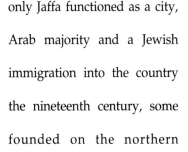

The early beginnings of the Rothschild Boulevard in 1910 in Ahuzat Bayit, later to become the nucleus of the city of Tel Aviv.

being one of them. The British, the new rulers of the country, granted these new Jewish neighborhoods an independent municipal status under the name of Tel Aviv ("Hill of Spring"), creating what has been known since as the "First Hebrew City." In those days, many of the creations of the Jewish population were known by the term "Hebrew" and not "Jewish": Hebrew settlements, Hebrew workers, Hebrew institutions. When the Hebrew city of Tel Aviv developed a new port at its northern end in the mid-1930s, it too was called a "Hebrew" port. It was built for the Jews of British Palestine, separate from the Arab port in Jaffa—following the emergence of Tel Aviv as a separate city from its Arab neighbor. When the State of Israel was established, however, and most of the Arab population of Jaffa left the country under the duress of war, the new Israeli government had the two municipal areas of Jaffa and Tel Aviv joined together as one municipality and named it Tel Aviv-Yafo (Yafo being the biblical Hebrew name for Jaffa).

Rise of a Center by the Sea Today, the city of Tel Aviv-Yafo functions as the most important economic center of the country and as the central focus of a large metropolis around it — the Tel Aviv metropolitan region. In the mid-nineteenth century, this region was mostly covered with sand dunes, sandy soils, some low hills of crystallized sand dunes (known locally as *kurkar*) and occasional fields of agricultural cultivation. By the end of the twentieth century, it became the most urbanized region in the country, inhabited by almost half of Israel's total population. Jaffa's origins were in antiquity and the town survived into the mid-nineteenth century as a tiny walled city on a little *kurkar* hill overlooking the Mediterranean Sea. It had a small port, primarily serving as a landing place for travelers on their way to Jerusalem. Its inhabitants were mostly Arab, with only a few Jews living in it at the time. As the country was gradually becoming a focus of interest to the outside world, Jaffa saw more and more travelers passing through it and paying for its services,

thus generating a process of urban growth. Christian pilgrims to the country increased in number and used Jaffa as a gateway to Jerusalem and other important Christian sites. In the last quarter of the nineteenth century, Jews were coming in larger numbers to settle in the country, and for them too Jaffa was the port of entry. Some of these Jews settled in Jaffa and played an

important role in building up the growing city's economic base and its port activities. More and more Jews were attracted to settle in Jaffa as they landed in the country toward the end of the nineteenth century. Jaffa served as a center for the new Jewish agricultural villages (*moshavot*) that had been founded on the coastal plain, not far from the town. The development of Jaffa as a rising economic center even attracted Jews from Jerusalem to come and join its nascent economic prosperity. Thus, during the second half of the nineteenth

Above: The port of Jaffa in 1910.

Below: Horse-drawn carriages waiting for passengers at the Clock Tower Square in Jaffa at the turn of the twentieth century.

century, the city on the coast emerged as a rival to the Holy City in the mountains. The competition Jerusalem experienced has intensified since then—first only with the city Jaffa, later with the twin cities of Tel Aviv and Jaffa and later yet with Tel Aviv-Yafo. Although Jerusalem is the capital of Israel and the chief attraction for tourists and pilgrims, the coastal rival has had the upper economic hand until this day. It is Tel Aviv-Yafo that has been serving as the main center for the economy and the arts in the country for more than half a century.

Growing Beyond the Walls of Jaffa In Jerusalem, urban expansion began in the mid-nineteenth century with the Old City walls remaining intact. In Jaffa, however, the walls were destroyed in 1863 to make room for contiguous expansion. They had become increasingly superfluous as a protective

measure against outside marauders and burglars. The camera came just in time to record the Old Jaffa walls before they came down in one premeditated act. The stones were used as construction material for the new development long contemplated by some of the city's more enterprising landowners.

Once Jaffa's walls had been dismantled, entrepreneurs were eager to exploit the empty land on the outskirts. Arabs and Jews began building homes and entire neighborhoods to accommodate the rising demand for residences there, as more and more people wished to escape the crowded alleys, the squalor and the lack of modern conveniences of Old Jaffa. The Jewish population was particularly active in this way, for reasons other than environmental. The Jews had mostly been renting their dwellings from Arab owners, who prospered

from this thanks to the growing Jewish immigration. Some Jewish entrepreneurs also wanted to benefit from similar arrangements by building new housing themselves. The new Jewish middle class in Jaffa was also anxious to build houses of its own in suburban locations as was being done in other parts of the country in those days. Moreover, as was the case in Jerusalem, Jaffa's

Jews strove to have neighborhoods of their own, where they could be their own masters — as some of their brethren already were in the Jewish agricultural villages that had been founded around the country in the previous decade. Thus, a new trend was set of building all-Jewish neighborhoods in the northeastern environs of Jaffa. While this was taking place, a major thrust of Arab neighborhoods was being constructed to the south and southeast of Old Jaffa, and not far from there German settlements were founded as part of a wider movement of German colonization in several places in the country. A new urban-rural mosaic emerged.

Jewish Tel Aviv by Arab Jaffa The first Jewish neighborhoods on the outskirts of Jaffa — such as Neve Zedeq and Neve Shalom — were mainly products of residential need. The next neighborhood to be established — Ahuzat Bayit, founded in 1909 — was initiated with national aspirations among a growing proportion of the Jewish population. The Jewish founders of Ahuzat Bayit saw it as a microcosm of the future national existence of the Jews in the country and, along with some of its newer neighbors, soon to be called

collectively Tel Aviv, as the forerunner of Jewish independence. This outlook characterized Tel Aviv for some decades and governed its relationship with Arab Jaffa. All along, the people of Tel Aviv were striving to build an independent Jewish realm of life in all its modern aspects: economic, cultural and political.

Tel Aviv has carried this message to this day, and has always surpassed Jerusalem in terms of modernity, worldly outlook and economic power. Very soon in its early decades, the Jewish Ahuzat Bayit suburb of Arab Jaffa, with its elegant homes and modern streets, disappeared from the landscape. Within just a few years, it became, somewhat reluctantly, the hub of a cluster of new Jewish neighborhoods. The first residents of Ahuzat Bayit had been opposed to the pursuit of any commercial activity within the quiet residential neighborhood. Even the regulations of the founding society ruled out any such activity, holding that Jaffa should be the economic base of the neighborhood. But the Jewish rush to the new northern areas overruled these expectations. The pro-progress and pro-development groups eventually prevailed and within two decades, what was supposed to be a garden suburb — after the fashion guiding the expansion of suburbs in Britain and North America — had turned into the commercial and administrative center of an emerging city. The British takeover of the country from the Ottoman Turks in 1917 opened up new opportunities for Tel Aviv. A surge of Jewish immigration accompanied the rising hopes for a Jewish national home, which were founded on the 1917 Balfour Declaration promising just that. This had dramatic influence on the growth of Tel Aviv. Many buildings were constructed there and roads were opened within a very short time, mainly on the shoreline toward the north, away from Jaffa. The extensive construction, however, did not provide enough housing. This and inability to pay high rents gave rise to a host of tents being set up in all corners of the new town — to provide shelter mainly for the recently arrived young Jewish immigrants. The scene at the time was quite hectic. New buildings were coming up along the sandy streets being paved, sand dunes were being flattened to make way for modern development, factories were producing bricks for construction and long convoys of camels were loaded with sand and bricks. And scattered in the midst of all this were the tents housing the young workers. This was a city in the making — aspiring to be a separate and autonomous Jewish city on the sand dunes, by the side of the Arab city of Jaffa. Progress was very quick. The new British government was sympathetic to the aspirations of the Tel Aviv neighborhoods' leadership and, in 1921, granted significant municipal autonomy within Jaffa. This took place only twelve years after the lots of Ahuzat Bayit were distributed among the founding members by a lottery, in a now famous gathering on the empty sand dunes in 1909. Eventually Tel Aviv was totally separated from the formal municipal ties with Jaffa to become totally independent and fully manage its own development. A series of violent outbreaks between Arabs and Jews — as a result of Arab opposition to the Jewish immigration and settlement — was not confined to Jaffa and Tel Aviv and spread periodically around the country. This only encouraged the completion of Tel Aviv's separation from its Arab neighbor. Many Jews, including business people, left Jaffa for Tel Aviv striking a new base in Ahuzat Bayit, particularly along Allenby Street (named after the British general who had led the takeover of the country from Turkish rule). By then, Ahuzat Bayit had become a busy commercial center for the Jewish population. The last of the violent outbreaks erupted in 1936 and lasted intermittently until 1939. Until that time, port activity was the only joint

Camels carrying sand on their backs for the construction of buildings in the new neighborhoods of Tel Aviv.

venture between the two cities. The 1936 outbreak, more violent than the former ones, led the Jewish leadership to opt for its own port in the then northern end of Tel Aviv. Port facilities were built and ships disembarked there to unload passengers and cargo. This, however, was not only a functional matter. The construction of an alternative port in Tel Aviv carried with it a heavy symbolic weight from a national point of view. The new port was to be a Hebrew port and was an object of great national pride and aspiration. The Jewish newsreels of the

In the early 1930s, Magen David Square on Allenby Street in Tel Aviv was already a busy urban center.

day made considerable efforts to depict it, photographers documented it and song writers lauded it as the first Hebrew port in the first Hebrew city. Although economically not such a great success, compared with the port of Haifa which was the main gateway to the country, the port of Tel Aviv expressed the total disengagement of the Jewish city from its Arab neighbor.

One City—Divided into North and South The Arab-Jewish war of 1948 and the establishment of the State of Israel that year created an upheaval in the fortunes of the two cities. They were merged into one, Tel Aviv becoming the prime focus of the enlarged city. New Jewish immigrants coming from the Middle East and post-Second World War Europe began settling mostly in Jaffa. The Arab population that had remained there was reduced to a small minority. New housing was built in many parts of the city, which now enjoyed a much larger municipal area, in all possible directions: north, south and east. The northern sections of town were primarily built to accommodate the emerging middle class, while the southern sections were mostly built with lower income housing to cater to the many immigrants. The clear division between a prosperous north and a proletarian south, which had already been noticeable in earlier years, became more distinct from the 1950s onward. The north-south pattern in the social geography of the joined city became an

Nahalat Binyamin Street in the 1920s, before it became a major commercial street of Tel Aviv.

underlying structure that would continue for years to come. The northern neighborhoods of Tel Aviv-Yafo quickly spread even further to the north. Many people aspired to reside in them. Some were themselves residents of the northern neighborhoods who wanted to move to a more spacious and more modern apartment than the one they had. Others were from localities around the country who came to Tel Aviv-Yafo to share in its prosperity and live in the better part of the city. They were joined by former residents of southern neighborhoods of Tel Aviv-Yafo who moved as soon as they became economically upwardly mobile. This movement of population from the south to the north further deepened the socioeconomic gap between the two parts of the city. This gap became increasingly evident in the built-up landscape. In the south there are many old dilapidated buildings, with cracked plaster and old paint, and with hardly any gardening around them. In contrast, in the north buildings are largely new and well kept, surrounded with trees and gardens. There are several boulevards in the north, but hardly any in the south. These contrasts in residential quality are also witnessed in the economic landscape. In the south there are many factories, workshops, warehouses and automobile repair shops, which do not add quality to adjacent residences. In the north, on the other hand, it is professional offices and commercial establishments that mingle with residences, in the same buildings or in separate ones. In recent years there have been some attempts to change the face of the southern areas. Some households and entrepreneurs have moved there to invest in real estate because the present lower values promise substantial future returns when both the building stock and the resident population are upgraded. The advantage of the southern neighborhoods is in their proximity to the city center combined with lower real estate values. Some find beauty in the old architectural style found there. The

municipality too is interested in the renewal of the old southern neighborhoods and encourages it in many ways. Substantial renewal efforts took place in recent years in the Neve Zedeq neighborhood immediately to the southwest of the business center of Tel Aviv-Yafo. It is one of the first Jewish neighbor-

Yehuda Halevi Street in the Ahuzat Bayit neighborhood in the 1910s. At the end of the street stand the houses of the older Jewish neighborhood, Neve Zedeq.

hoods built at the end of the nineteenth century to the north of Jaffa. In its early years, the Jewish elite of Jaffa lived in Neve Zedeq. There were merchants and bankers as well as authors and artists. However, as the Jewish city of Tel Aviv spread to the north further away from hostile Arab Jaffa, this elite moved northward and in its stead came increasingly less affluent households. Eventually Neve Zedeq joined the rather large strip of poor southern neighborhoods. But a century after its establishment the neighborhood again saw well-kept homes of the well-to-do. In the beginning only a few pioneering households took up the challenge of settling in a poor and deteriorated neighborhood. When it became clear that the first ones succeeded and the value of their property appreciated substantially, others joined in and renovated more of the old dilapidated houses. Local residents watching their neighborhood improving have themselves begun to take part in the renewal process and set out to invest in their houses rather than move out of the neighborhood. Today Neve Zedeq has made a name for itself in neighborhood renewal, not only in Tel Aviv-Yafo but throughout Israel's cities. In Tel Aviv-Yafo the pioneering efforts of this neighborhood has shown the way to other ones nearby.

Center of a Metropolis The growth of the city and its neighboring suburbs, such as Ramat Gan and Petah Tiqva to the northeast, Holon, Bat Yam and Rishon Leziyyon to the south and southeast and Ramat Hasharon and Herzliyya to the north, had a significant impact on its central areas. Business activities spread through them extensively, taking over many of the numerous residences that had been inhabited even in the 1950s and 1960s. Many of the former residents moved further away to the newly built outlying neighborhoods, while some left the city to take up more comfortable and less expensive residences in the suburban cities around. The businesses gave rise to the construction of tall office buildings all over the central areas, the result of which has been a complete transformation of the city's skyline. Formerly, the planners of

For many decades Tel Aviv was characterized by low-rise buildings. Coffee shops and restaurants are clustered along the seaside promenade.

Tel Aviv vetoed construction of buildings higher than three or four floors. Thereby, for many years, Tel Aviv had a relatively low and flat skyline, unlike the norm for decades in numerous cities of its size around the world. But with time and with the pressure of market demand, the planning code was changed. In the last decades, the skyline has been completely transformed, scattered with high-rise buildings, piercing the sky and claiming a place for Tel Aviv in the array of modern metropolitan centers around the world. The claim to a share in the modern urban world is not so recent. In the 1920s, when it was realized that Tel Aviv was emerging as the main Jewish center in the country (although it was, at the time, a town of fewer than twenty thousand inhabitants), some of the entrepreneurs involved in construction were particularly ambitious in their vision of the city's future. They ventured to draw up plans for urban buildings, rich in architectural content and substantial in size — far beyond its earlier image as a cozy and comfortable garden suburb. The architectural message of the 1920s was sustained through time in some of the older buildings in the heart of the city. Later, ambitious vision dwindled giving way to mundane and unimaginative residential construction characteristic of the 1950s and 1960s. In the 1970s, the area with the most intense development of high-rise buildings was where Ahuzat Bayit and the other early neighborhoods of Tel Aviv had originated. The first tall office building to be constructed, thirty-four floors high, was the Shalom Tower. It stands over Herzl Street, one of the main streets of Ahuzat Bayit. At the outset of the neighborhood, its most impressive building was the Herzliyya Gymnasium (High School) where many of the first generations of youngsters from Tel Aviv and the Jewish settlements in the vicinity were educated and inducted into the country's Jewish elite and intelligentsia. This succumbed to redevelopment in the early 1960s and the school was moved northward to join the residential shift of the middle class. At the time, there was not yet an awareness among the inhabitants of Tel Aviv of the value of old architectural and cultural landmarks and there was no notable public outcry—just a sigh of lament following the disappearance from sight of a landmark that was so firmly

associated with the cultural life of early years in Tel Aviv. The Shalom Tower (built instead of the Herzliyya Gymnasium) heralded a new phase in the life of the city, an age of intensive business closely interlinked with world economy and gradually paralleling other metropolitan centers of the world. The transition from school to office building symbolizes effectively the transforma-

tion that has taken place in the city's landscape and in the nature of its economy and society. A similar transformation can be seen along the seaside of Tel Aviv. In its early years, Tel Aviv was rather oblivious to the enviromental and cultural value of its proximity to the sea. High-class residential areas did not compete then for seaside locations as they now do. On the contrary, there was a time, from the 1920s to the 1950s, when obtrusive factories stood on the shoreline, as well as poor neighborhoods that included clusters of shacks. There was no dignified promenade for those residents of the city and out-of-town visitors who wanted to stroll in the breeze and enjoy the horizon over the sea. For years, much of the city's sewage was dumped into the sea immediately in front of designated beaches, frequently polluting the Mediterranean

Above: The new city hall of Tel Aviv in the 1930s. The municipality since moved its offices to much larger premises.

Below: In the 1920s, Lilienblum Street in Tel Aviv was aligned with fashionable residences. It is now part of the financial center of the city.

Sea. For a long while, the was uninterested or only seaside had to offer. Almost all were established far from the were amenable to it, such as in

Jewish society in the country slightly interested in what the the new Jewish settlements sea, even when circumstances Herzliyya or Hadera. This was

the case in Tel Aviv too. But those times are over. For some decades now, many changes have taken shape along the seaside. The rise of tourism to the country has led to the construction of a string of fashionable hotels along the shore of the Mediterranean Sea, some of which are owned by world-renowned hotel chains. A carefully designed promenade has been paved along the shoreline in recent years and is a source of pride to the residents of the city. In all, there has been a substantial change along the seaside, although there are always two sides of the coin when it comes to landscape transformation. Some see it as a sign of improvement; others view it as a loss. Many lament the loss of the view due to the hotels and the disappearance of natural landscape along Tel Aviv's shoreline; others commend the intensity of urban life along the interface between city and sea.

Left: The town of Jaffa in 1895, viewed from the north. The town itself is built on a hill near the Mediterranean Sea. The port on the right served in the nineteenth century as the main entry to the country, especially to Jerusalem.

Below: Old Jaffa, a view from the north a century later. Much of Old Jaffa on top of the hill was cleared to make room for an archaeological garden.

Top: The monument commemorating the 1909 founding of Ahuzat Bayit, the small neighborhood which grew to become the core of the city of Tel Aviv.

Bottom: The spring of 1909 gathering of the Ahuzat Bayit association members for the lottery by which the land parcels of the future Jewish neighborhood were distributed. The gathering took place on a sandy area northeast of Jaffa.

Left: Nine decades later, the large city of Tel Aviv-Yafo is built on the former sandy areas along the Mediterranean coast. The site of the historic lottery gathering is located at the intersection of Rothschild Boulevard and Nahalat Binyamin Street.

Top: Herzl Street in the early years of Tel Aviv was initially built as a residential street. The building of the Herzliyya Gymnasium (high school) stood at its head. The street itself was still unpaved. A horse-drawn carriage served the transport needs of the new neighborhood. Most of the inhabitants worked and shopped in Jaffa.

Bottom: A traffic policeman in the middle of Herzl Street in the 1920s.

Herzl Street nowadays is one of the busiest streets in the center of the city of Tel Aviv-Yafo. At its head is the Shalom Tower, a commercial and office building. On some of its side streets are tall bank buildings. Along the street are many stores, specializing mainly in clothing and furniture.

Above: Rothschild Boulevard in Ahuzat Bayit in 1910, one year after the establishmant of the new Jewish neighborhood. Many houses were already standing on both sides of the boulevard, which was still under construction. No trees were as yet planted. The old Jewish neighborhoods Neve Shalom and Neve Zedeq established over two decades earlier, are seen further away. Two passenger boats are anchored in the sea near the port of Jaffa.

Opposite: Rothschild Boulevard in the 1990s is a major business street in the center of Tel Aviv-Yafo. Tall commercial buildings have risen on both sides of the boulevard, replacing the old residential homes built in the early years of Ahuzat Bayit.
The trees along the boulevard have grown too, and now fill the street with lush shades of green. Beyond the boulevard are the red roofs of Neve Zedeq neighborhood, which has lately been undergoing intensive upgrading and gentrification.

Top: Parallel to Rothschild Boulevard, on the south, runs Yehuda Halevi Street. For many decades this part of Yehuda Halevi Street was flanked by a railroad track connecting the port of Jaffa with Jerusalem. The train seen in the 1946 photograph enters the railroad station on Yehuda Halevi Street further to the right.

Bottom: Today tall buildings lining Yehuda Halevi Street serve as headquarters for many banks. The railroad tracks are long gone as is the railway station. The cleared spaces were turned into parking areas.

Opposite: The Ahuzat Bayit streets now form the central business district of Tel Aviv-Yafo. The intensity of the urban landscape is a far cry from the sandy area of 1909. Yehuda Halevi Street runs from the lower left to the upper right and intersects Allenby Street. Further to the left is Rothschild Boulevard.

Below: The city of Tel Aviv has stretched along the seashore north of Jaffa, and interacts with the sea in various ways. A view of Tel Aviv from the hill of Old Jaffa in the 1920s reveals that Tel Aviv's skyline was still low and no promenade ran along the seashore. In the foreground lies the al-Manshiyye Arab neighborhood of Jaffa, and further to the upper right is Ahuzat Bayit.

Right: As Tel Aviv was spreading northward it drew closer to the seashore, and tried to make use of it by building promenades, bathing beaches, seaside parks, coffee shops, restaurants, and hotels. This is evident in the view of Tel Aviv from the hill of Old Jaffa in the late 1990s.

*Further north of Ahuzat Bayit, additional Jewish neighborhoods were built on the sand dunes,
on both sides of Allenby Street, (named after the British general who headed the armies that conquered
the country from the Ottomans in 1917-1918). The street ran northwest from Ahuzat Bayit to the
Mediterranean shore. In 1914 Allenby Street was still a dirt road used by a convoy of camels proceeding
toward the seashore to pick up sand for the construction of Tel Aviv's new buildings.
In the foreground one can notice that in this part of the emerging city construction was quite sporadic.
Many of the workers lived in tents, due to a shortage of housing and unaffordable prices. Jaffa and its port
are seen in the distance. The minaret of the Hasan Bek mosque marks the northernmost Arab neighborhood
of Jaffa – al Manshiyye.*

*By the end of the 1990s, Allenby Street near the seashore is part of the densely built urban landscape
of Tel Aviv-Yafo.*

*Opposite: Another view of the streets that have been built between Allenby Street and the
Mediterranean sea.*

Right: The square at the end of Allenby Street was named after Herbert Samuel, the first High Commissioner of British Palestine. A photograph of the early 1930s shows the square and the coastal strip north of it. In those days automobile traffic was not permitted along the shore, which was reserved for pedestrians only. Taxis and horse-drawn carriages still competed for passengers. In later years a building was erected on the corner near the carriage station. The Knesset held its first sessions there, before moving to Jerusalem.

Bottom: In 1921 the Tel Aviv beach near the end of Allenby Street was in its early making.

Opposite: The Herbert Samuel Square continued to change its face to this day.

Top: An aerial view of Tel Aviv and its beaches in 1937. The Mahlul neighborhood, with its wooden huts hastily constructed to house Jewish refugees from Arab Jaffa, is situated directly over the beach. The city itself extends over a large area between the sea and the agricultural areas to the east. The German colony Sarona is in the left background. Most of the buildings of Tel Aviv were still only of three to four floors high. On the beach bathers sit in rows of beach chairs lined up parallel to the sea.

Opposite: Sixty years later there is no trace of the wooden huts of the Mahlul neighborhood. They gave way to tall hotel buildings. Other high-rise buildings mark the present landscape of the city. A fully-fledged promenade extends along the beach.

Center: A view of the seaside of Tel Aviv in 1957. A park, a promenade and some beaches extended along the shores of the Mediterranean Sea.

Bottom: Another view of the hotel strip on the Tel Aviv shoreline.

Top: Zina Dizengoff Square is one of the famous landmarks of Tel Aviv. It was named after the wife of the first long-time mayor of the city, who was also one of its founders in 1909. In 1934 the square was only delineated by a dirt road. The area immediately adjacent to it was not yet built.

Center: Zina Dizengoff Square in 1939 was almost fully built, the buildings around it adjusting their design to that of the square. There was already gardening within the square itself, and trees were growing around it. The four-story building on the other side of the square housed the Esther cinema and the Eckman mini-department store, both well known in Tel Aviv and its region at the time.

Bottom: In the 1990s the fountain in the center of Dizengoff Square was redesigned and became an art piece.

Opposite: Dizengoff Square in the 1990s is a major landmark in the urban landscape of a city about to change its face, due to the proliferation of high-rise buildings.

Below: The present city of Tel Aviv-Yafo started in the small port town of Jaffa, still surrounded by fields and groves.

Right: Urban development moved rapidly to the north as far as Kikar Hamedina (Hamedina Square) and then crossed the Yarqon river (in the background) where high-rise residential buildings have recently been built, primarily for the upper-middle-class population.

The Coastal Plain

With the city of Tel Aviv-Yafo lying in its center, Israel's coastal plain is now the most developed and most urbanized part of the country. The coastal plain stretches from south of the city of Haifa in the north to the town of Ashqelon in the south and includes many of the country's large cities and towns. Many of these places were established as *moshavot*, the private version of the early Jewish agricultural settlements. Some of these *moshavot*, such as Petah Tiqva, Rishon Leziyyon and Hadera, were founded in the last quarter of the nineteenth century.

Planting the first tree on the main street of Rishon Leziyyon around 1884.

Others such as Herzliyya and Netanya were established in the 1920s and 1930s when Jewish settlement in the country accelerated. Some towns, such as Lod (Lydda) and Ramla or Yavne and Ashqelon, were formerly inhabited by Arabs and were settled by Jewish immigrants following the 1948 upheaval. Since then these towns have expanded far beyond their old original core. Both Lod and Ramla had a small Arab population in 1948; these now reside largely in neighborhoods of their own. Some towns, such as Ashdod and Qiryat Gat, have their origin in the wave of urban construction that followed the establishment of the State of Israel and the onset of mass immigration of Jews. The founding of new urban settlements continued in the coastal plain in later decades. Most of them are planned as relatively small communities, such as Kokhav Ya'ir on the foothills of the Samarian mountains, while Modi'in, is currently being built as a large city half way between Tel Aviv-Yafo and Jerusalem. On the eastern margins of the coastal plains Arab towns, such as Taiyibe and Tireh, are growing out of their former rural origin. Their population has increased considerably in recent decades and new neighborhoods have been added to the original rural core. Altogether the map of cities and towns in the coastal plain is considerably diverse. This reflects on the one hand the historical order in which new urban forms were shaped from time to time and on the other hand the social and cultural variety of the Israeli population.

The rural settlements in their various forms add further diversity to the settlement map of the coastal plain, a region of intensive rural settlement. It is the largest lowland region in the country, rich with fertile and cultivable land, where deep ground water is most ample. The first historical layer of rural settlement in the coastal plain was the Arab villages scattered in many parts of the region but particularly in its southern section.

Only a few of these villages remained after 1948, almost all of them along the eastern margins. The second layer is the *moshavot*, most of them now towns, but a few, such as Giv'at Ada or Mazkeret Batya, still keep their rural character. Gradually, some of these *moshavot* developed into commercial urban centers, and later even added industrial activities to boost their economic structures. Although the older areas of these *moshavot* had preserved most of their original rural landscapes in the early days of statehood, they too were soon undergoing transformation. Detached homes, which had been built by

individual families when the villages were largely farming communities, gave way to new apartment buildings, and later even to office buildings. The once rustic appearance of the village streets was lost to an urban style. Nowadays, it is hard to believe that many of the busy urban streets of Rishon Leziyyon or Kefar Sava were once quiet rural lanes, where horses pulled carts loaded with farm produce and where children could play with little interruption by traffic. The loss of the rustic look is also due to the disappearance of fruit orchards and vegetable gardens, which had covered the expanses of the agricultural villages. Many of the old houses had been surrounded by sizable plots of land, on which the farmers could pursue a variety of agricultural activities. There had even been several farm structures in the fields, such as cow sheds and chicken coops, as well as storehouses for the produce and the farming equipment. All these are long gone in many of the now urbanized *moshavot*. Here and there, a few of the old farm structures remain standing in a corner, next to a large apartment building, as a reminder of what had been. Besides these few remainders, the cow sheds

Above: Hadera in the 1940s is an urbanizing moshava.

Below: Kevuzat Yavne, a kibbutz in the southern coastal plain.

and the farming equipment can now be seen in the family album, the history book, the private collection and the local history museum. A third layer of rural settlements on the coastal plain is the numerous *kibbutzim* and *moshavim* scattered all over the region. Many of them were founded during the British

period, interspersed between the existing *moshavot*. Others such settlements were formed in the early 1950s, when the new state had plunged into an ambitious project of attracting new immigrants to the rural-agricultural way of life, with an eye to securing the state's territorial hold around the country, particularly in areas with a relatively sparse Jewish population.

In the decades that followed the huge settlement wave of the 1950s across the coastal plain, the main process that shaped the map of establishments on the plain was suburbanization. All over the region, small villages as well as larger towns were becoming destinations for households looking for less expensive, more spacious and more comfortable housing. This wave of suburbanization started in regions close to the Tel Aviv metropolis and gradually spread to areas further afield. As the demand for suburban residence increased among the Jewish urban population, many of the relatively new settlements were taken over by this process and gradually changed in size and character. In recent years, many *moshavim* have gradually been transformed from rural agricultural communities to suburban locales, from which many residents now commute to the big city, having chosen to join these settlements and the new neighborhoods currently being added to some of them for more spacious living in a detached house with an adjoining garden.

In all, the various processes of establishment that have taken place on the coastal plain have produced a dense continuum of Jewish settlement between Hadera in the north and Ashqelon in the south, centering on the metropolis of Tel Aviv. As one town borders the other, there is hardly a distinction between what is urban, rural or suburban. Nevertheless, three major regions within the coastal plain can be historically and geographically identified: the Tel Aviv metropolitan region, the Sharon plain to the north (including the Carmel coastal plain) and the southern coastal plain to the south. The boundaries of the Tel Aviv metropolis keep changing as it spreads outward to add more places to its economic system.

THE TEL AVIV METROPOLIS The pivot of the intensive urbanization in the coastal plain was the ever-growing city of Tel Aviv. As it grew larger in size and in economic scope, it had an impact on the

Vineyards on the outskirts of Petah Tiqva in the 1890s.

surrounding Jewish settlements. Tel Aviv became the hub of economic growth, enabling the nearby *moshavot* to commercialize their agriculture and even introduce industry, using the economic services of the large city as an anchor. In contrast, the *moshavot* in other regions of the country, notably those in Galilee in the north, have lagged behind, continuing as rural communities to this day. Tel Aviv's growth set in motion a process of suburbanization, leading to further population growth and economic development in nearby *moshavot*. The central division of the coastal plain evolved as one large metropolitan region, with Tel Aviv as its focus. Young families, in search of more spacious dwellings than they could have afforded in Tel Aviv proper, have settled in nearby towns, which originated in *moshavot*. Factories requiring large tracts of land, which were no longer available or too expensive in Tel Aviv, moved to the towns on the close and distant perimeters. In this way, *moshavot* like Herzliyya to the north of Tel Aviv, Petah Tiqva to the northeast and Rishon Leziyyon to the southeast have emerged as large suburban cities, from which many of their residents commute each morning, to work and for other purposes, to Tel Aviv.

Petah Tiqva The city of Petah Tiqva, in the northeastern part of the Tel Aviv metropolis, is the first of the early generation of *moshavot* established by Jews at the beginning of modern Jewish settlement in the country. Its transition from a small agricultural settlement not far from the southern bank of the Yarqon river, can serve as an interesting case study in tracing the changes which took place in those *moshavot* drawn into the sphere of urban development centered on Tel Aviv-Yafo. Petah Tiqva was founded in 1878 by a group of religious Jews, who had left the Old City of Jerusalem to build a new economic base in agriculture and rural life. Until then, the Jewish population in the country had been concentrated in a few urban areas, the most important of them being Jerusalem, Hebron, Tiberias and Zefat. It is noteworthy that the first attempts to establish new rural Jewish settlements in the country were made by old-time Jewish residents. This fact is contrary to the more familiar image portraying newcomers from abroad, largely from Europe, as the only originators of Jewish rural settlement in the country. Being the first, and a rather successful attempt, Petah Tiqva is called the "Mother of the *moshavot*." It was the first of its kind and similar to the ubiquitous type of rural settlements around the world: villages founded on private property and individual farms established within. The early days of Petah Tiqva were quite harsh. The site originally stood on the southern bank of the Yarqon, a small river, flanked with swamps on both sides, which were infested with malaria. Moreover, the sandy soils of the region could not support a flourishing agricultural enterprise. Relief and change came with the introduction of citrus cultivation to the *moshavot* of the coastal plain, Petah Tiqva included. The sandy soils, when combined

In 1971 the urban landscape of Petah Tiqva had hardly any trace of its rural past.

with modern fertilizers and new deep water drilling technology, introduced in the 1920s, provided a framework for agricultural prosperity based on the export of citrus fruits and products to Europe. The citrus economy was more than just agriculture. It supported a large number of workers in industry, transportation, commerce and services, as well as in agriculture itself. As a result, Petah Tiqva and other *moshavot* on the coastal plain, attracted from the early 1920s many new residents, a large number of them new immigrants, all striving to partake in the growing citrus-based economy. Very soon, Petah Tiqva ceased to be a village and became a town — one of the largest among the urbanizing *moshavot* of the coastal plain. Eventually, as in other urbanizing *moshavot*, its growth was no longer based primarily on the citrus economy. Other industries moved there in search of less expensive locations than in Tel

Aviv. Moreover, as Tel Aviv was growing into a metropolis, Petah Tiqva was becoming a residential suburb of the central city. Young families in particular were starting out in Petah Tiqva, where they could afford to purchase an apartment or house and avoid the rising real estate prices of Tel Aviv and even Ramat Gan.

A dramatic change took place in Petah Tiqva and the other *moshavot* of the coastal plain after 1948, with the advent of mass Jewish immigration into the country. It was well placed for the absorption of many of the immigrants. The economic opportunities of the emerging Tel Aviv metropolis were close by, and being a former agricultural settlement, land for residential construction was

Above: Young orange groves in Kefar Sava around 1930. Below: Herzliyya in the late 1930s.

ample. New immigrant housing projects were built on its outskirts. The phenomenal population growth of those years was shared by many towns and cities around Israel, but Petah Tiqva took a generous share of that growth. Since the 1960s, Petah Tiqva and other *moshavot* which evolved as suburbs of Tel Aviv-Yafo have continued to attract people and economic enterprises. This process has had some major effects on the landscape of these towns. The built-up area has expanded to create new neighborhoods and industrial zones—but many orchards were the victims of this expansion as they were cut down and buildings constructed in their place. In the inner neighborhoods, where the *moshava* once stood, old detached houses with tile roofs, huge old trees and gardens at their sides have been demolished, and given way to modern high-rise residential buildings. All these dramatic changes began less than five decades ago, when Petah Tiqva was still known as a *moshava*. Now, this fact is only a matter to be studied in history books. In Petah Tiqva, the **now** has completely taken over the **then**, as well as the **in between**. Today, Petah Tiqva is a city of over a hundred and fifty thousand inhabitants. Its main streets look like many of the streets of Tel Aviv, only lacking some high-rise office buildings. It will probably gain some soon.

The Southern Sharon *moshavot* The changes that took place in Petah Tiqva were repeated in one way or another in its neighboring *moshavot* in the southern Sharon which nowadays forms an integral part

of the Tel Aviv metropolis. Kefar Sava today looks very different from what it had been in the early 1920s. Then, only a few small houses were scattered along the yet unpaved road, among fresh saplings too young and too small to bear fruit for export. Now, its tall urban buildings rise over the rolling plain. The main street of Ra'anana, formerly the only one in the budding *moshava*, has

drastically changed since the late 1920s. Once a long farmers' lane, unpaved and aligned with small houses that headed lengthy agricultural plots, it is now a shopping street boasting supermarkets, department stores and offices and stretching over a mile. Similarly, the city center of Herzliyya, which had been the original area of the *moshava* established in the late 1920s, is now a major business center, densely built up with tall residential buildings. Only along its edge can one still spot a few family homes that have survived since the early years. New family homes, detached and semi-detached, have more recently been built on the margins of these towns. In recent decades, while more and more tall apartment buildings have been built in the centers of the *moshavot* near Tel Aviv, middle-class families have increasingly opted for houses of their own, with small gardens attached. The search for a 'villa' or 'cottage' has become so prevalent recently, that many of the new neighborhoods beyond the Tel Aviv region have been built specifically to provide this kind of housing. Ra'anana, Herzliyya and Ramat Hasharon, just north of Tel Aviv and close to the Mediterranean Sea, have been leading towns in this new trend.

Rishon Leziyyon Established in 1882, Rishon Leziyyon was one of the forerunners of the new Jewish *moshavot*. Like other *moshavot*, it embraced the guidance and support of the Baron Edmond de Rothschild administration and soon adopted vine growing as one of its major agricultural pursuits. Rishon Leziyyon became home to the main winery in this part of the country, gathering the grapes

A street in Rishon Leziyyon in 1910. The moshava is still in its rural phase.

grown in the south to manufacture wine products. Its early leaders had envisaged an urbanized future for their settlement, striving to be the first "Hebrew" city in the country. The geographical setting and the course of history, however, led to other realities. The early Jewish neighborhoods in the north of Jaffa were soon to assume the leading role in urbanization and formed Tel Aviv as the urban center of the Jewish population; Rishon Leziyyon was to preserve its rural character for some time to come. In 1948, when Tel Aviv-Yafo was already reaching a quarter of a million inhabitants, Rishon Leziyyon's population barely exceeded ten thousand. Nevertheless, continuous immigration to Israel induced urban development in Rishon Leziyyon, which soon joined the growing metropolis of Tel Aviv. Its rural, agricultural past proved beneficial. Its large tracts of land, some of them utilized for vineyard and citrus cultivation, increasingly gave way to urbanization. As the town was quickly growing into a city, the sand dunes west of the city and aligning the shores of the Mediterranean Sea proved to be a sizable reservoir of space for extensive housing developments. By the end of the twentieth century, Rishon Leziyyon is far from its rural origins and is approaching a population mark of a hundred and seventy thousand. This process was clearly reflected in the transformation of its landscape. High-rise residential buildings were constructed in the center of town, as well as on the urban edge. Industrial areas were built to the north and northwest. The original area of the *moshava* soon turned into a dense and highly active commercial center serving the needs of its inhabitants. Yet, with all this growth, Rishon Leziyyon is primarily a suburban city and an integral part of the Tel Aviv metropolitan region. Every day Rishon Leziyyon sees many commuters journey to the hub of the metropolis.

Ramat Gan Not only the working class approached the suburbs of Tel Aviv to look for affordable housing, but also some members of the middle class, who were searching for a less dense residential environment, did the same. On the rolling hills to the east of Tel Aviv, the city of Ramat Gan ("Garden

Heights") began its development in the 1920s. At first, its character reflected the original concept of a "garden city" as a suburban alternative to the large city. But soon, as more people came to reside in the Tel Aviv region, Ramat Gan grew to become one of the largest cities in the country. Its leaders were very ambitious about their city. They were not satisfied with only residential growth

The Qiryat Avoda neighborhood in Holon, 1937

and were anxious to introduce first industry and later commerce and business, and to compete with Tel Aviv as a primary business center. Nowadays, adjacent to the eastern municipal boundary of Tel Aviv, tall office buildings—including Israel's diamond exchange—mark the skyline of Ramat Gan, giving it the image of a city doing business with the rest of the world, just as its older sister, Tel Aviv-Yafo, has been doing for some time.

Benei Beraq On the hilly topography east of Ramat Gan, the city of Benei Beraq currently presents a dense urban environment, in which a large population of Haredi (ultra-orthodox) Jews live. It has now reached the dimensions of Ramat Gan in population and is crowded with *yeshivot* (Jewish religious seminaries), catering to students who come from all parts of the country and even from abroad to study. But Benei Beraq was not a busy urban center some decades ago. It started in the 1920s as an agricultural settlement, as did some of the "newer" *moshavot* to the north of Tel Aviv, such as Herzliyya and Ra'anana. Right from the start, it catered to religious Jews and for over two decades maintained its rural character. Then, in the 1950s, Haredi Jews began to congregate in Benei Beraq, making it their preferred town in the growing Tel Aviv metropolis. Many of them came out of Tel Aviv itself, which until then had been the region's primary center for the Haredi population. Tel Aviv-Yafo was thus reduced to a minor setting for this community's residence.

Bat Yam and Holon The process of suburbanization beyond Tel Aviv has included areas other than the *moshavot*. In the 1930s, along the seashore south of what was then the Arab city of Jaffa, two small Jewish suburban communities were established: Bat Yam and Holon. They heralded the suburbanization of the Jewish working class, which could not afford the soaring prices of real estate in Tel Aviv itself. New immigrants filled these two towns after each immigration wave in the early decades of the State of Israel as well as in the early 1990s, when many new immigrants from the former Soviet Union settled in them. Nowadays the sand dunes of Bat Yam and Holon have been covered with large built-up areas, housing hundreds of thousands of residents.

THE SHARON North of Tel Aviv-Yafo and Petah Tiqva lies the Sharon region, now one of the most settled parts of Israel's coastal plain. Toward the end of the nineteenth century, the area was only sparsely populated with small Arab villages and Beduin encampments. Since then, however, the Sharon region has witnessed Jewish settlement and intensive agricultural development. For many years, it was one of the richest agricultural regions in the country, primarily active in citrus cultivation. The light, sandy soils that covered most of the Sharon proved suitable for the production of citrus fruits, particularly oranges. During the 1920s and 1930s, huge areas of the Sharon were planted with citrus trees, assisted by plentiful ground water, which was discovered by deep drilling, and modern fertilizers. Soon, large expanses of the Sharon, once consisting of uncultivated land that had occasionally been used for grazing, was transformed into a green landscape of intensive agriculture.

Zikhron Ya'aqov In the north of the Sharon stands one of the region's earliest *moshavot*. Zikhron Ya'aqov was founded in 1882 on the southern edge of the Carmel mountains. After a few years of hardship, its settlers, like many in other *moshavot*, requested to join the philanthropic support system of Baron Edmond de Rothschild of Paris. The Rothschild administration assisted the *moshavot* for about sixteen years, during which financial help and professional guidance were provided to the farmers. Similar to other *moshavot*, most of Zikhron Ya'aqov was built aside a long street, then called the "farmers' street," where the farmers kept their

houses and farmyards. This street was crossed by a shorter one, then called the "administrators' street," along which the buildings of the Rothschild administration were located. The Baron's administration encouraged the Zikhron Ya'aqov farmers, as it did in other *moshavot*, to develop a vineyard agriculture and a wine industry. Vineyards were planted in Zikhron Ya'aqov and in its neighboring *moshavot*, which had by then emerged, such as Bat Shlomo, Giv'at Ada and Binyamina. A large winery was built in Zikhron Ya'aqov itself,

Top: Swamps in the Hefer valley in 1925, before Jewish settlement in the region.

Bottom: Kibbutz Ma'abarot in the Hefer valley in 1938, five years after its establishment.

Left: The main street in Zikhron Ya'aqov in 1912.

making it the center of the wine industry in the region, even to this day. With time, however, farming ceased to constitute the dominant branch of Zikhron Ya'aqov's economy. Its cool air and the delightful views of its surroundings, particularly that of the Mediterranean coast, began to attract resort establishments and in the 1950s, immigrant housing projects were added to its outskirts. Since the 1970s, suburban commuters have settled in the small hilly town, as it is also conveniently located near the major Haifa–Tel Aviv highway and the sea.

The Northern Sharon *moshavot* This trend of opting to live in smaller places quite far from the large cities brought many new residents to the cluster of small *moshavot* in the northern Sharon. Among them are Pardes Hanna and Karkur, which are now under one municipality and located not far from Hadera, the capital city of the northern Sharon and itself one of the earliest *moshavot* in the country. Many of the commuters living in the small towns and villages in the northern Sharon work in Hadera, a city of over sixty thousand inhabitants, or use its services. The arrival of these commuters added a new look to the small

The khan in Hadera, formerly an Arab farm, was the first base for the Jewish settlers in Hadera in 1890.

moshavot in the Sharon — and such places across the coastal and cottages have gradually had once covered large areas a process also took place not for that matter, to many other plain. White-washed villas superseded the orchards that in the northern Sharon. Such far from Tel Aviv-Yafo. These houses, forming new neighborhoods on the outskirts of the *moshavot*, have taken over the landscape, which had once been characterized by farm houses in the core of each settlement and some workers' or immigrant neighborhoods in its periphery. Hadera was established as a *moshava* in 1891. The first settlers found shelter in what they called the *khan*, a large farm building constructed earlier by the former Arab landlord. Their main obstacle was an outbreak of malaria, prevalent in the nearby swamps. The early years of Hadera were plagued by this disease and many of the settlers died or were chronically fatigued. But with time, the swamps were drained and medical teams aided in stopping the disease. Hadera grew to become a prosperous town, combining citrus agriculture, commerce and some industry. Located half way between Tel Aviv and Haifa, it attracted many immigrants in the 1950s, and since the 1970s, its population has grown with the arrival of commuters, who work in the larger cities along the coast between Haifa and Tel Aviv. Hadera's once rural core is now a densely built-up urban landscape. Its old rural homes have mostly disappeared.

Netanya and the Central Sharon *moshavot* The city of Netanya, south of Hadera, is presently one of the largest cities in the Sharon, attracting a great number of commuters and shoppers from its vicinity. It lies on the shore of the Mediterranean Sea and is populated by over a hundred and fifty thousand inhabitants. Not long ago, however, it was but a small *moshava* aspiring, like other *moshavot* in the Sharon, to prosper on citrus growing. Founded in 1929, almost four decades after Hadera, by 1948 it had equaled the

size of its older sister and in the mid-1990s, had surpassed Hadera considerably. It is now far from its rural beginnings. The leaders of the *moshava* quickly recognized its potential for urban expansion based on industry and a seaside resort. Many hotels now line Netanya's seashore, attracting a large number of

The main street of Netanya in the 1930s. Netanya was soon to become a thriving town.

tourists from abroad each summer to bathe in its Mediterranean waters. Netanya, more than any other city in central Israel, made the seaside economy a prime basis for its livelihood — a fact well reflected in its garden and beach landscape alongside the streets facing the sea. Another city that has maximized its economic potential in coastal tourism is nearby Herzliyya, where numerous hotels grace the seashore as well as some of the city's prestigious neighborhoods. Southeast of Netanya, in the mid-Sharon plain, lies another cluster of settlements which originate in *moshavot* founded during the British period: Even Yehuda, Kefar Yona, Qadima and Tel Mond. For years these *moshavot* remained in their initial rural layout, encompassed by extensive citrus orchards. In the 1950s new immigrants were added as new residents to these small places affecting the social balance between farmers and workers, between old-timers and newcomers as well as between Ashkenazi Jews and Jews from Muslim lands. But this social change did not bring about a change in their rural character.

The distance from the Tel Aviv metropolis was still an important factor in those years and most of those leaving Tel Aviv for the suburbs were content with the *moshavot* of the southern Sharon, such as Herzliyya and Petah Tiqva, which were much closer. Since the 1980s, as more people moved to the suburbs, the value

Even Yehuda, a small moshava in the Sharon in 1938.

of land in the southern Sharon soared, and consequently the mid-Sharon settlements began to attract new residents from among the middle-class population in search of a house of their own in a rural or semi-rural setting. This started with a tiny stream of newcomers but in the 1990s the trend has accelerated. Following the wave of immigration from the former Soviet Union, the central government hurried to change the zoning of substantial areas in the periphery of the metropolis from agricultural to residential land use. New neighborhoods were soon built in many suburban towns and villages instead of fields and orchards.

Moshavim and kibbutzim in the Sharon Scattered in clusters over the Sharon plain, between the smaller and larger *moshavot*, are many *moshavim* and *kibbutzim*. The first round of this kind of settlements was established between the 1920s and the 1940s, most of them taking part in their early years in the already expanding citrus agriculture. A contiguous area of *moshavim* and *kibbutzim* is found in the

Kibbutz Sedot Yam on the Mediterranean Sea in 1951.

Hefer valley that lies northeast of Netanya. In this rolling valley, that had almost no Arab settlement, the Jewish national institutions purchased a large tract of land and allocated it to Jewish settlement of a cooperative nature — *moshavim* and *kibbutzim*. Among the first of these settlements was Kefar Vitkin,

now on the side of the coastal highway running between Haifa and Tel Aviv-Yafo, a major transportation artery in the Sharon. But in its early days, in the 1930s, Kefar Vitkin was quite far from any paved road. In the early 1950s, many immigrant *moshavim* were founded in the Sharon, especially in its eastern margins, close to the foothills of Samaria. They experienced meager beginnings, its settlers living in small houses and largely depending on agriculture. However, in recent decades, many of their residents have taken on urban employment and, lately, with the increasing preference for low density living, some city people have opted to rebuild their lives in the suburbanizing countryside. Nowadays, many of the *moshavim* in the Sharon, as well as other parts of the coastal plain, look very different from their modest beginnings. The small farm houses have been replaced by spacious suburban villas encircled by well groomed gardens, and it is often difficult to discern where the town ends and the countryside begins. The village has turned into a suburb.

Arab Settlements on the Eastern Margins On the eastern margins of the Sharon, beyond the row of *moshavim* and *kibbutzim*, lies a string of Arab towns and villages, such as Umm el-Fahm, Baqa el-Gharbiyye, Taiyibe and Kafr Kassem. They represent the ancient line of settlement running along the western foothills of the Samaria mountains. In 1949, as a result of the armistice between Israel and Jordan, these Arab areas were placed within the borders of Israel. Not long ago, they were just small villages, depending largely on agriculture. In recent decades, however, some of them have evolved into small and medium sized towns, from which many commute to work in the larger cities nearby: in the Tel Aviv metropolitan region, in Netanya or in Hadera. Taiyibe, for instance, located northeast of Tel Aviv, was a small village of five thousand residents in 1950. By the mid-1990s, its population had reached twenty-five thousand. While the construction of modern buildings and paved streets has transformed the newer parts of Taiyibe into a somewhat urban landscape, the older areas have maintained their old and traditional appearance.

New Suburban Settlements New suburban communities in the Sharon region are primarily places of comfortable residence. Largely consisting of detached homes and most of them staying small in population, some stand out as islands of prosperous living. The new settlement of Kokhav Ya'ir, between Kefar Sava and Taiyibe, is one such example. It was first settled mostly by people connected with Israel's security forces, who have a long experience in building suburban settlements and residential neighborhoods noted for their environmental and social qualities. Nearby, along the eastern margins of the Sharon plain, similar new suburban settlements are being developed — Zur Ig'al, Zoran and Bat Hefer, being some examples. They have become the primary vehicle of new settlement and development on the country's periphery in the past two decades, taking over from the *moshavim* and *kibbutzim* that were previously performing this national task.

THE SOUTHERN COASTAL PLAIN South of Tel Aviv lies the region of the coastal plain known in earlier decades as the South, the Lowland of Judea or the Judean Plain. Nowadays, it is a nameless region but is one of the most urbanized parts of Israel. We shall call it here the southern coastal plain. Like the Sharon, it is one of the most settled parts of the country. There is a dense network of small and medium sized towns in the region, some originating in older settlements that existed before the State of Israel was established while others were established later. As in other parts of the country

The main synagogue of Rehovot at the turn of the twentieth century.

outside the long-standing cities, modern Jewish settlement in the southern coastal plain originated in a cluster of *moshavot*. These were established south of the city of Jaffa toward the end of the nineteenth century. The better known among them are Rishon Leziyyon and Rehovot, which are now fully-fledged cities and a far cry from the small agricultural settlements they had been over a century ago. In recent decades the Tel Aviv metropolis has spread to encompass Rishon Leziyyon. For the purpose of following the transformation in the country's landscape Rishon Leziyyon is included in this volume within the framework of the Tel Aviv metropolis. Following these two owns, but quite far behind in terms of population, is the town of Nes Ziyyona, between Rishon Leziyyon and Rehovot. Further from Rehovot are the small towns of Be'er Ya'aqov to the northeast and Mazkeret Batya (once known as Eqron) and Gedera to the south. Today, these are urban localities of several thousand inhabitants — but not long ago, they were large villages.

Rehovot Rehovot was established in 1890, south of Rishon Leziyyon. It too started as an agricultural settlement, at first planting vineyards and exporting wine. Later, the citrus industry became the primary segment of its economy. Its small winery evolved into a factory for the production of citrus juices and other

citrus-based canned products, and served as a source for later industrial development. Meanwhile, large-scale

citrus growing brought many agricultural workers to Rehovot.

A group of Jews from Yemen arrived in Rehovot in the early

twentieth century to work in its agriculture and settled in a

neighborhood of their own on the southern outskirts of the

already sizable *moshava*. Sha'arayyim, as it was named, was not

the only one of its kind in the *moshavot*. Other Yemenite neighborhoods had been founded on the outskirts of

many earlier *moshavot*, among them Hadera and Petah Tiqva. The Jews from Yemen, arriving in the country in

larger numbers since 1882, lived in homogenous clusters and maintained their unique Jewish culture for some

time. Later, as Rehovot expanded—mainly after 1948, when many immigrant housing projects were built on its

periphery—Sha'arayyim was fully integrated within the built-up area of the town. It is now very close to the

commercial center of Rehovot, where tall buildings have replaced the original rural homes of earlier decades.

Besides being a commercial center, Rehovot has evolved as the focal point for some major academic

institutions. It houses the Weizmann Institute, which concentrates on scientific research, and the Faculty of

Agriculture of the Hebrew University. Alongside these operate many research and high technology industries.

The Small *moshavot* of the Southern Coastal Plain Some of the *moshavot* in the

southern coastal plain did not follow the usual course of rapid urbanization and for a long time remained

small. The rural appearance of Nes Ziyyonna, Gedera and Mazkeret Batya long revealed their origins as

moshavot. Many of the houses built at the turn of the twentieth century persevered in these *moshavot* while those

in the rapidly urbanizing *moshavot* had long been replaced by large apartment buildings. Until the 1970s the

main change in the small *moshavot* was the addition of housing for immigrants on the outskirts. Their original

core continued to look like a *moshava* and in fact is so called by the local residents. But as the zone of influence

of Tel Aviv-Yafo further expanded in the coastal plain, the turn of the smaller *moshavot* to enter the process of

change arrived. Change took place in two main ways: in the original core of the *moshavot* tall apartment

buildings replaced the old family homes while on the outskirts new villa neighborhoods were developed.

Moshavim and *kibbutzim* in the Southern Coastal Plain The region is densely

dotted with *moshavim* and *kibbutzim*, quite a few of them founded between the 1920s and 1940s. Some of

these settlements spread further south of the old *moshavot* and, during British rule in the country, extended the line of Jewish settlement southward. These southernmost settlements proved crucial for the defense of the new state in 1948, when it was at war with Egypt and other Arab countries. Some of the *kibbutzim*—Negba among them—prevented the Egyptian army from moving in from the south. In the aftermath of the war, after almost all the Arab population of the southern coastal plain had left as refugees to other destinations, mainly to the Gaza Strip, new Jewish settlements were added to the region, particularly further south, close to the Negev. Among the many new Jewish immigrants arriving in the country in the early years of statehood, some ventured to establish new agricultural settlements, mostly *moshavim*, while others were directed to make use of the evacuated Arab towns, such as Lod and Ramla, close to Rishon Leziyyon and Rehovot in the north of the southern coastal plain, or to Yavne and Ashqelon further south a long the coast.

New Towns in the Southern Coastal Plain During the 1950s and 1960s many of the immigrants of those years populated the new towns established in the southern coastal plain, such as Ashdod, Qiryat Malakhi, Sederot, Netivot and Qiryat Gat. These new towns were part of a grand scheme prepared by the Israeli government, immediately after the state was formed, to establish a series of new towns, mostly in the outlying regions of the country. The purpose of this scheme was to settle many of the immigrants away from the densely populated areas of the

country, particularly the Tel Aviv metropolis. The scheme was part of a general government policy to disperse the Jewish population to areas on the country's periphery in order to increase Jewish presence there. This policy had both political and planning motives. On the one hand, there was a need to strengthen

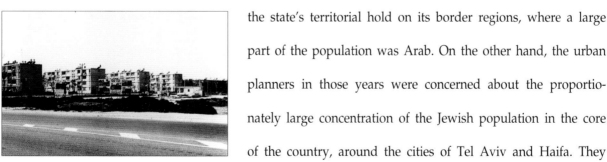

the state's territorial hold on its border regions, where a large part of the population was Arab. On the other hand, the urban planners in those years were concerned about the proportionately large concentration of the Jewish population in the core of the country, around the cities of Tel Aviv and Haifa. They were anxious to prevent the majority of the immigrants from settling in that core, which would cause increased congestion and the loss of fertile agricultural land to residential construction. The first step within the framework of this policy was the establishment of several hundred immigrant *moshavim* across the country. The southern coastal plain received a large share of these *moshavim* and was soon covered by many settlements, where new immigrants learned the skills of agriculture. Most of the towns established a few

Above: Moshav Bet Hannan in 1930, the year of its founding, near Nes Ziyyona.

Left: The new town of Qiryat Malakhi in 1965.

years later in the region were placed in the midst of the new agricultural settlements, with the intent that these towns would function as commercial and service centers for their rural neighbors. It was soon realized that these towns, growing in population as immigration continued, had to develop an additional economic base in order to support their residents. Thus, in the late 1950s, industrial plants were established in most of the new towns across the country, textile factories taking the lion's share of this development. Hence, in each of these towns a new industrial zone emerged, which provided most of the local employment opportunities.

Ashdod Although it came under the population dispersal scheme of new towns, the town of Ashdod managed to become one of the largest cities in the country, due to the fact that it was founded in 1956 as a port city on the Mediterranean Sea. Ashdod is now approaching the mark of a hundred and thirty thousand

inhabitants and is home to the busiest port in the country. In the early 1950s, it was just a stretch of sand dunes lying some twenty-five miles south of Tel Aviv-Yafo, until its port was built to replace the small and outdated port facilities existing in Old Jaffa and in the north of Tel Aviv. In the decades following, Ashdod was continually populated with immigrants arriving in the country.

Ashdod in its first years— in the early 1960s.

The wave of immigration from Morocco in the early 1960s brought many new residents and the immense wave of immigrants from the former Soviet Union in the first half of the 1990s added tens of thousands of residents within five years. New neighborhoods were quickly added to the southern parts of the city and now hardly a sand dune can be found in its immediate vicinity which is not covered with new buildings.

Qiryat Gat in the Lachish Area Further toward the interior of the southern coastal plain, the town of Qiryat Gat was established in the mid-1950s. It was planned as the urban center of the Lachish area, a region which was populated during that time by a series of Jewish settlements, most of them *moshavim* founded by new immigrants. Qiryat Gat, like Ashdod, absorbed many immigrants from Morocco and from the former Soviet Union and now houses about fifty thousand residents in neighborhoods that cover a large area on the rolling plain. In its first years, it was characterized by modest sized residential buildings, but with time, its urban character became more defined and now tall residential buildings imprint the city's skyline. This is markedly noticeable as one nears Qiryat Gat from the major highways that approach the town from all four directions. Surrounding Qiryat Gat are the green fields and orchards of the many agricultural settlements of the Lachish area, which thrive on the supply of water brought from the north via the national water grid developed in the country in the early 1950s. The landscape in the Lachish area today represents a remarkable contrast to the one that existed in pre-State years. Now the area is densely settled and cultivated intensively. The story of the southern coastal plain's landscape transformation is twofold. On one hand is the substantial but gradual change that took place in the early Jewish settlements — mostly the *moshavot*. On the other is the abrupt and marked transformation that took place within a very short time following the establishment of the State of Israel in 1948. It transpired as almost all the Arab population living there prior to that year left the region under the duress of war and Jewish immigrants settled in new rural and urban

settlements. This abrupt change was particularly dramatic in the southernmost parts of the coastal plain, where Arab settlement had been rather sparse due to the semiarid conditions and Jewish presence minuscule. Within less than a decade, scores of the Jewish settlements filled the rolling plain and intensive cultivation transformed the barren landscape. A network of new towns was also added to the region.

Above: Building the Afridar neighborhood of Ashqelon on the Mediterranean Sea in 1951.

Left: The Afridar neighborhood of Ashqelon in 1997.

Top: One of the main streets of Petah Tiqva in 1910, more than three decades after it was founded as the first Jewish moshava in the country in 1878 – Hovevei Ziyyon Street at the corner of Montefiore Street.

Bottom: In 1997 Hovevei Ziyyon Street in Petah Tiqva is at the center of a city of over one hundred and fifty thousand inhabitants. Its former rural character was completely transformed into an urban one. The city of Petah Tiqva is now an integral part of the Tel Aviv metropolis.

Top: A convoy of camels in the 1930s, on what is now Kefar Gannim
Road in Petah Tiqva. The southern outskirts of the moshava were
cultivated with various kinds of orchards. The earlier vineyards were
replaced with citrus groves.

Bottom: Kefar Gannim is nowadays a prestigious neighborhood in the
southern part of Petah Tiqva. The orchards were replaced by spacious
villas and cottages.

Top: The main street of Ra'anana, a moshava in the southern Sharon, northeast of Tel Aviv, in the late 1920s. Ra'anana was one of the citrus based moshavot built in the Sharon Plain after the First World War. Most of Ra'anana in its early years was built along this one main street.

Bottom: The main street of Ra'anana, one of the cities of the Tel Aviv metropolis, in 1997. The urbanization of Ra'anana has been accelerated in the last three decades of the twentieth century, when many new villa neighborhoods were built on its outskirts, and apartment buildings rose along its main street replacing the old rural houses of earlier decades.

Top: In 1925 Kefar Sava, a moshava northeast of Petah Tiqva, was
still struggling to become a viable place.

Bottom: In 1997 the moshava of Kefar Sava is already a fully-fledged
city of over seventy thousand inhabitants.

Top: Herzliyya in 1938, thirteen years after its establishment in 1925 as a citrus-based moshava in the southern Sharon, still had its original rural character. Note the water tower on the hill, so characteristic of many Jewish settlements in those days. Herzliyya was named after Theodor Herzl, the founder of the Zionist Organization.

Bottom: Herzliyya in 1997 is one of the largest cities in the Tel Aviv metropolis. Tall apartment buildings have risen in its old center, and on its periphery. The water tower of the old days still stands.

Top: The western part of Herzliyya, not far from the sand dunes along the Mediterranean shore in the early 1930s. The photograph was taken from the north facing south, from what would later be the site of Kefar Shemaryahu, a village to be established in 1936. Note the dirt road on the right. Further to the right are the seaside sand dunes.

Bottom: The western part of Herzliyya in 1997. In the foreground are the houses of Kefar Shemaryahu, now a prestigious suburb with expensive homes. The old dirt road is now the main coastal highway of the country, running between Haifa and Tel Aviv-Yafo. The entire western part of Herzliyya, known as Herzliyya Pitu'ah, is now densely built-up and reaches the seashore on the right, which is lined with a string of tall hotels.

*Above: The cliffs along the shoreline in the west of
Herzliyya in the early 1930s.*

*Opposite: Hotels, restaurants and other installations of a
modern bathing beach line the shore of Herzliyya
in 1997. The western edge of the city is now one of the
most developed tourist areas in the country.*

Rishon Leziyyon in the late 1890s, from the west. At the end of the main street, on top of the hill, stands the main synagogue of the moshava. The large building to the left (north) of the main street is the headquarters of the Baron Rothschild administration, which in those years supported and managed the economy of Rishon Leziyyon and many other moshavot around the country.

Opposite: The core of Rishon Leziyyon along Rothschild Street in 1997. The village has long turned into a sizable city.

Loading wine barrels on camels at the Rishon Leziyyon winery in the 1890s.

The orchestra of Rishon Leziyyon parading in the main street in 1912.

124

*Right: Shekhunat Borokhov, the first
neighborhood of the future city of Giv'atayyim
in the 1920s, when it was a nascent workers'
suburb on the eastern outskirts of Tel Aviv.
Shekhunat Borokhov was the first such workers'
neighborhood in the country.*

*Above: Shekhunat Borokhov is now an integral
part of the middle-class city of Giv'atayyim,
adjacent to Ramat Gan.*

Left: Ramat Gan in the early 1920s was a budding suburb on the hills northeast of Tel Aviv. Its founders in 1921 wanted the new settlement to be a "real garden city," when it was realized that Tel Aviv was going to become a very urban place.

Above: Urbanization caught up with Ramat Gan as well. Eight decades later, in 1997, Ramat Gan is part of the contiguously built core of the Tel Aviv metropolis, with over one hundred and thirty thousand inhabitants.

Opposite top: Benei Beraq celebrating its first year in 1924. A gate is spanned next to the main road connecting Tel Aviv with Petah Tiqva, at the entrance to Rabbi Akiva Street, now the main shopping street of the town.

Opposite center: Benei Beraq in 1933.

Opposite bottom: Raising dairy cattle was one of the main agricultural activities in Benei Beraq in its early years.

Above: In 1997 Benei Beraq is a city of over one hundred and thirty five thousand inhabitants, most of them orthodox and ultra-orthodox Jews. Many yeshivot – religious seminaries – are concentrated in the core of the city.

Bat Yam was established immediately south of the Arab city of Jaffa in 1926. Its name up to 1937 was Bayit Vagan. In 1950, when this photograph was taken, Bat Yam was still a tiny suburban community by the Mediterranean Sea, known primarily for its beaches. The port of Jaffa in the near background and the port of Tel Aviv further away still functioned then.

*In 1997 the beach of Bat Yam is flanked by tall residential
and hotel buildings. Bat Yam grew to become a suburb of over one
hundred and forty thousand inhabitants in the southern part
of the Tel Aviv metropolis.*

Right: The Arab town of Ramla in 1917, during the war between Britain and the Ottoman Turks. A military unit is encamped in tents near the town.

Below: The town of Ramla eight decades later is a growing suburb in the Tel Aviv metropolis.

Bottom: Ramla in the late 1890s.

Top: Plowing vineyards in Zikhron Ya'aqov in the late 1890s.

Center: The winery of Zikhron Ya'aqov in the late 1890s.

Bottom: The winery of Zikhron Ya'aqov in the late 1990s.

Left: The water tower was the pride of the small moshava of Karkur in the northern Sharon. Plenty of ground water was found in the area in the 1920s.
The photograph was taken in 1926.

Right: In recent years villas and cottages have been built in Karkur, now part of the municipality of Pardes Hanna-Karkur.

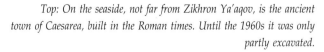

Top: On the seaside, not far from Zikhron Ya'aqov, is the ancient town of Caesarea, built in the Roman times. Until the 1960s it was only partly excavated.

Bottom: The cleared moat and the restored fortifications of Caesarea as viewed in 1997.

Right: A view of ancient Caesarea and environs in 1997. The town of Or Aqiva is in the far background.

Opposite Top: A street in Hadera in 1997 when it is already a fairly large town in the northern Sharon.

Opposite Center: A street in Hadera in 1914, when it was still a small agricultural village.

Opposite Bottom: Yemenite pupils and their teacher in the Yemenite neighborhood of Nahliel on the northern outskirts of Hadera in 1914.

Below: A general view of Hadera in 1997.

Top: Netanya, a small moshava in the Sharon, on the Mediterranean Sea in the early 1930s, a few years after its establishment in 1929. The large building with a dome is the main synagogue. The sea is beyond the edge of the cliff.

Bottom: Netanya, a city of one hundred and fifty thousand inhabitants, seven decades after its establishment.

Top: The coastal cliff and the beaches of Netanya in the 1930s.

Bottom: In 1997 Netanya's built-up area reaches the edge of the cliff. The beaches attract many visitors and tourists. Many of the buildings by the sea are hotels.

Top: Kefar Vitkin, a moshav in the Hefer valley of the Sharon, in its early beginnings in 1935.

Bottom: In 1997 Kefar Vitkin is a prosperous agricultural village.

Top: Moshav Bet Yizhaq near Netanya in the Hefer valley in 1940. The area around it is rather empty. In the distance one can see a few new Jewish settlements being developed.

Bottom: In 1997 Bet Yizhaq looks more like a comfortable suburb than an agricultural village. Its short distance from Netanya attracts commuters to take up residence in the moshav.

Top: Many new Jewish settlements were added to the coastal plain north of Tel Aviv-Yafo.
One of them was Habonim, a communal moshav founded in 1949 near the seaside,
west of Zikhron Ya'aqov, on the site of a former Arab village.
In a picture of the early 1950s one can see behind Habonim a train passing on the recently
built coastal railroad between Tel Aviv-Yafo and Haifa. The Mediterranean Sea
is further in the background.

Bottom: Moshav Habonim in 1997.

Top: A view of the newly established immigrant moshav named Porat in the mid-Sharon region near the moshavot of Qadima and Tel Mond. The photograph was taken early in 1951. The first settlers in Porat came from Libya.

Bottom: A view of Moshav Porat in 1997. The farmers specialize in growing flowers in greenhouses and exporting them to Europe.

Opposite: Rehovot in 1997 is a city of eighty-five thousand inhabitants and many tall buildings.

From Top to Bottom:
Rehovot was established in 1890 as one of the early moshavot located on the coastal plain south of Jaffa. The photograph shows the new settlement in 1897.

Rehovot's main street in 1912 was still unpaved. The synagogue stands on the hill in the background.

Farmers posing for the camera in Rehovot in the late 1890s.

A donkey-drawn cart on the main street of Rehovot in 1933.

Top: A horse-drawn carriage passing near the moshava of Nes Ziyyona in 1910. Nes Ziyyona was settled by the first Jewish farmer in 1882, north of Rehovot.

Bottom: Nes Ziyyona about nine decades later is a medium sized town situated between its two larger neighbors: Rehovot to the south and Rishon Leziyyon to the north. It is on the verge of becoming a fully-fledged suburb in the Tel Aviv metropolis.

Top: Gedera, a moshava south of Rehovot at the end of the 1890s. Gedera was founded in 1884, south of Rehovot.

Bottom: The old renovated core of Gedera in 1997 is now a comfortable small town, with spacious homes and tall trees, a far cry from its early beginnings.

Top: Kibbutz Negba, founded in 1939 as one of the outlying Jewish settlements in the southern coastal plain, protected itself in its first days with a "Tower and Stockade," common in settlements founded in the late 1930s. Trucks were carrying additional materials to be used in the construction of Negba's buildings.

Bottom: Kibbutz Negba after a few years. The water tower still played an important role in the defense of Negba in the 1948 War of Independence, and now stands as a monument to an heroic act of defense.

Opposite: Kibbutz Negba in 1997. Note the water tower in the center of the settlement.

Top: The new town of Ashdod was founded in 1957 on the sand dunes to the south of the Tel Aviv metropolis. The photograph shows one of the first residential quarters in 1958.

Bottom: Ashdod was planned to be the major southern port of the country, to replace the outdated small ports of Jaffa and Tel Aviv. The photograph shows the residential area near the port in 1964.

Top: Ashdod grew into a major city of one hundred and thirty thousand inhabitants in 1997, covering a large area of the former sand dunes. Many immigrants from the former Soviet Union have settled recently in the newly built quarters of Ashdod.

Bottom: The residential area near the port is now one of the better neighborhoods of the city of Ashdod.

City of Haifa

The Mediterranean city of Haifa, on the slopes of Mount Carmel, is now the largest urban center in northern Israel. Today, it lies in the middle of a metropolitan region that stretches along the coast and penetrates far

inland. The city's development industrial output and role as and the adjoining valleys. touching on the Mediterranean Mount Carmel. The city,

is due to its major port, large a commercial hub of Galilee Haifa's urban landscape, Sea, is now dominated by first on the plain, climbed,

with time, from the shore to the top of the mountain. This expension only began in the mid-nineteenth century. Although Haifa has its roots in antiquity, it never grew to any substantial size until the mid-eighteenth century. At that time, the shallow port of Acre, lying to the north of Haifa bay (formerly known as the Acre bay) ceased to accommodate the larger sea-borne vessels. As a result of Acre's decline, its port functions were transferred to the small fishing village of Haifa, where the waters were deeper than in Acre. This move had historic impact on the entire region. Acre gradually lost to Haifa its position as the main port city in the region and although in the mid-nineteenth century Haifa was still a small town surrounded by walls, clinging to the sea, it was soon on its way to modern development. It began to reach out beyond its walls to the immediate surroundings, in a pattern similar to the developments in Jerusalem and Jaffa at the time. An important boost to the development of Haifa came with the arrival of Germans from southern Germany. They lived in a settlement they had built for themselves outside the walled city in 1868. The German Colony

in Haifa, as it came to be such settlements established by members of the Temple Christian community, who virtue of a deeply religious

known, was one of a group of around this time in the country Society (*Tempelgesellschaft*), a came to the Holy Land by motivation. Haifa's German

Colony, with its spacious houses and well-planned main street, was not only a modern addition to the traditional landscape of this walled city, but also brought with it modern economic development. The German settlers improved the port facilities, paved the roads leading inland, primarily for horse-drawn carriages traveling to Nazareth, and founded the necessary services to cater for the increasing numbers of pilgrims and tourists who were landing in Haifa on their way to the various attractions in the country. The German settlers in Haifa, with the help of the German Kaiser who visited the country in 1898, were able to convince the Ottoman government to link the port of Haifa with the new railroad system running between Damascus and the important Hejaz region in the Arabian Peninsula. This materialized at the beginning of the twentieth century and Haifa gradually emerged as a major center of transportation in the Levant. New factories were founded in the city, along with new commercial enterprises, and very soon, people flocked to join its new prosperity. The Jewish community responded by increasing its presence there through immigration from abroad and migration from other parts of the country. Consequently, from a tiny minority living alongside the Arab

The Herzliyya neighborhood on the slopes of Mount Carmel in Haifa in the 1910s.

inhabitants within the walls of the Old City, the Jews quickly grew in numbers and inhabited new neighborhoods on the outside. Their first neighborhood, Herzliyya, was sited on a broad terrace on the lower slope of Mount Carmel in 1912. This initiated a pattern of spatial movement around Haifa. The Jews later spread out high on the slopes of Mount Carmel, while the Arabs left the walled city to more immediate areas on the seaside, next to the port. Although Jewish and Arab residential developments tended to be geographically separate — the Arabs in the lower city and the Jews in the upper city—Haifa remained one and did not split into two municipalities, as had been the case between Jaffa and Tel Aviv. The terrace on which the first Jewish neighborhood outside the Old City

was built was also the site of the first Jewish institute of technology, known as the Technion. Founded in 1913, it heralded the important economic role that Haifa was soon to take on as a major industrial agglomeration in the country. The Technion building soon became an architectural landmark for which Haifa was known for

The Bat Galim neighborhood at the foot of Mount Carmel in Haifa in the late 1920s.

many years, until a new campus was built further out on the slopes of Mount Carmel in the 1950s. Another turning point in the modern development of Haifa was introduced with the advent of the British in the country at the end of the First World War. They made the city the gateway to this part of the world. Immediately embarking on an ambitious project to build a large, modern deep-water port in Haifa, the British invested great efforts to reclaim land from the sea to enlarge the deck area of the port. The project was completed in the early 1930s and Haifa's economy and urban development was boosted by port-related activities. A new business center emerged behind the newly built port, making Haifa a modern city, a far cry from the small provincial town that it had been just a few decades earlier. The port and the commercial and industrial areas adjoining it had become prominent elements in Haifa's landscape, which could be seen as one

approached the city from the sea or looked upon it from the top of Mount Carmel. Such scenes were particularly favored by professional and amateur photographers who followed the rapid growth of Haifa with their cameras. Mount Carmel was no longer a mountain covered with trees and bushes. Large tracts on its slopes and even its crest were covered with sprawling

Hadar Hakarmel neighborhoods in Haifa in the 1930s.

urban neighborhoods. The original Old City was, by the late 1930s, but a small section of the total city. The small Herzliyya neighborhood was by then a large residential quarter by the name of Hadar Hakarmel, where a Jewish commercial center evolved, in addition to the one near the port. The small Ahuza community on top of the mountain was the kernel of a string of Jewish neighborhoods built aside the main road running along the mountain crest. During the 1920s, Jewish groups, looking for more reasonably priced housing,

Top: The Haifa railroad station in the 1910s.

Bottom: A horse-drawn carriage on the seashore road between Haifa and Acre in the 1910s.

moved to new suburban towns built on the sandy plain backing onto Haifa bay. Each of these towns catered to a particular sector of the Jewish population. Qiryat Haim, for instance, was settled by workers affiliated with the Labor Federation (*Histadrut* in Hebrew). The neighboring Qiryat Bialik was founded by middle-class immigrants from Germany. Gradually, this suburban region of Haifa covered wide expanses of the formerly

empty plain. The rest of the sandy plain was built up with heavy industry and refineries and the smoke rising from their chimneys became an integral, albeit not so pleasant, part of Haifa's landscape. The refineries, like the new port, were built by the British, who had designated the city to be the terminal of the major pipelines carrying crude oil imported from Iraq.

In 1948, war broke out between Arabs and Jews. The flow of crude oil to Haifa was stopped and British rule in the war-ridden country was terminated. Most of the Arab population left during the war and Jewish immigrants settled in their stead. Haifa ceased to be an important terminal at the head of the Middle Eastern pipeline and railroad network. Nevertheless, the city

recovered soon after the war. Some of the older parts of the city were torn down to give way to new development and on the outskirts of the city new housing estates were built for a mixed population of immigrants and old-timers. The port activities were soon resumed, making Haifa the major port of the country for some time—until the port of the new city of Ashdod in the southern coastal plain was built and soon became the country's busiest port. With time, as the population of Haifa grew, additional neighborhoods were built on the slopes of Mount Carmel and over its crest, covering the mountain with a solid built-up area. In spite of the extensive construction, Haifa has kept its charm. The juxtaposition of sea and mountain has bestowed upon the city a unique beauty. It has a large port and substantial industrial areas, but at the same time it has tourist and resort attractions—one of them being the magnificent Bahai temple overlooking the city from the upper slope of Mount Carmel. The neighborhoods on top of the mountain enjoy a pleasant climate and a breathtaking view of the sea and coastal strip. Here is situated the new Haifa University campus. Standing tall, the university tower acts as a modern beacon seen from far away in Galilee.

Haifa is not only visually connected with the north of the country. The city serves as the main economic and administrative center of the northern region. Many Jews as well as Arabs, who live all over the north, are commercially, socially and culturally tied to the city.

A view of the Hadar Hakarmel section of Haifa on the slope of Mount Carmel in 1997.

Right: Haifa is a modern city in the late twentieth century (1996). Its built-up area rises to the top of Mount Carmel. Haifa port is one of the major ports on the Mediterranean Sea.

Below: A view from the bay of Haifa and Mount Carmel in the early twentieth century. The town lay near the sea and on the lower slopes of the mountain. Its port was small and was mainly engaged in local fishing.

Right: A narrow street in Old Haifa in the late nineteenth century.

Below: In the 1930s Khamra square in Lower Haifa is a hub of transport. The horse-drawn carriages still compete with the newly introduced automobile.

Opposite: A general view of Lower Haifa in 1997. In recent years new office buildings have risen over the older buildings of the commercial area near the port and the nearby railroad yards.

Top: German farmers in the German Colony of Haifa in the late nineteenth century.

Bottom: The German Colony in Haifa in the early twentieth century.

Right: A view of the German Colony in Haifa in the late twentieth century. The Bahai temple is now in the foreground.

Opposite Top: A view of Haifa and its bay from the northeast in the early twentieth century. The port grew to serve the increasing traffic to and from the country. Within the country, however, transportation from Haifa to Acre was still on camels and carts, using the sand beach along Haifa bay.

Opposite Bottom: Haifa and its bay in the late 1920s after the British authorities had built a modern port in Haifa and constructed a long jetty. The large building in the foreground is the Technion, an institute of technology established in 1925 in the Jewish district of Hadar Hakarmel.

Below: Haifa and its bay in the late 1990s. The city now extends over the entire slope of Mount Carmel. The old Herzliyya neighborhood, later known as Hadar Hakarmel, is now the core of a large city.

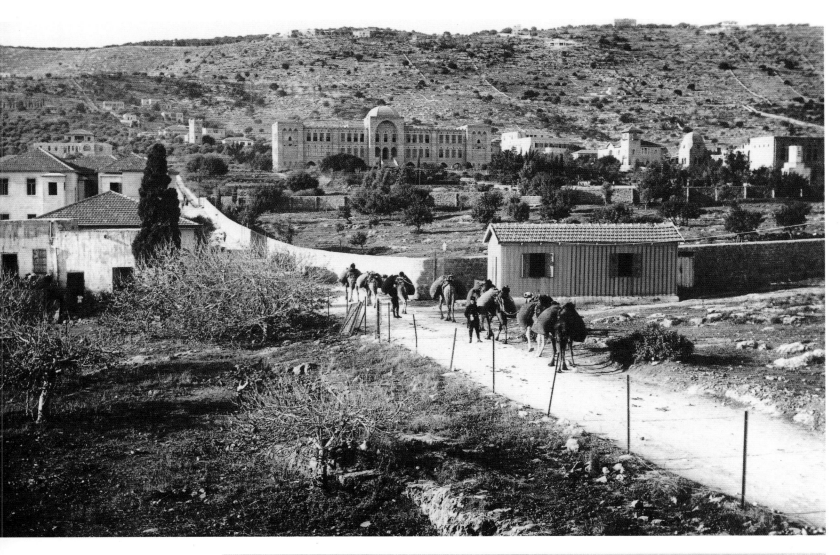

Opposite Top: The old Technion building in Haifa in the late 1920s. There were already some residential buildings on top of Mount Carmel.

Opposite Bottom: A view of the new Jewish neighborhoods of Haifa on the lower slope of Mount Carmel in the early 1920s. Old Haifa with its minarets is close to the sea.

Top: The old Technion building and the Hadar Hakarmel district of Haifa in 1997, facing Lower Haifa and the port in the background.

Bottom: The old Technion building and the Hadar Hakarmel district of Haifa in 1997, facing Mount Carmel in the background.

*Top: Herzl Street in the Jewish district of Hadar Hakarmel in Haifa in 1925.
At that time it was still a residential street.*

*Bottom: In the 1990s, Herzl Street is a main shopping street in the
commercial center of Haifa.*

*Right: Celebrating the festival of Shavu'ot on Herzl Street in the Hadar Hakarmel district
of Haifa in the early 1930s.*

Opposite Top: Nordau Street in Hadar Hakarmel, Haifa, was a quiet street with grand homes in the 1930s.

Top: Nordau Street in Haifa in the 1990s.

Opposite Bottom: A view of the Hadar Hakarmel district of Haifa in the 1940s. Hadar Hakarmel is built on a terrace on the middle slope of Mount Carmel. The Mediterranean Sea is in the upper left of the photograph. In the center is Gan Binyamin, a city park on Nordau Street.

Bottom: A view of Gan Binyamin in Hadar Hakarmel in 1997. Many of the middle-class residents of Hadar Hakarmel have moved away to newer neighborhoods in the city, some to the new neighborhoods on Mount Carmel.

680. Paysan des environs de Caïffa.   Bonfils

Haïfa — Mount Carmel and Bath Galim

Opposite Top: A Druze elder traveling on a donkey on the road leading out of Haïfa to the west, around Mount Carmel. In a photograph from the 1880s one can see the Carmelite monastery of Stella Maris on top of Mount Carmel.

Opposite Bottom: The Jewish neighborhood of Bat Galim was built in the 1920s, between Mount Carmel and the Mediterranean Sea, along the road leading west out of Haifa. By the 1930s, the Stella Maris monastery has an additional new building. Its first building was built in 1827.

Above: Bat Galim in 1997. Mount Carmel is in the background.

Top: A view of the southeastern neighborhoods of Haifa and the plain at the head of the Haifa bay in the 1930s.
Note the extensive areas of sand dunes stretching inland from the seashore. One of the ravines flowing down from Mount Carmel is spanned by a bridge.

Left: Modern bridges now connect both sides of the mountain ravine in southeastern Haifa. The Haifa bay area is in the background.

Top: In the 1930s a series of new towns was built on the sandy areas near Haifa bay, northeast of the city. Among them were Qiryat Haim, Qiryat Bialik, Qiryat Motzkin and Qiryat Shmu'el. The entire area came to be known as Haqerayot.

Bottom: The built-up area of Haqerayot by the Haifa bay now extends over a sizable part of the plain between Haifa and Acre.

Galilee and its Surrounding Valleys

The northern region of Israel combines two types of geographic features. The mountainous core, known since antiquity as Galilee, is encircled by valleys on three sides: the Jordan valley on the east, the Harod and Jezreel valleys on the south and the Zebulun valley and the Acre plain, along the Mediterranean seashore on the west. Over the centuries, Galilee and its surrounding valleys have witnessed many settlers, including Jews who densely populated more so during the Hellenistic centuries the northern part of peoples and religions in various towns and walled cities. This the region in biblical times and and Roman period. For many the country was a mosaic of types of settlements: villages, kind of cultural mosaic existed in the northern regions also in the middle of the nineteenth century, prior to the onset of modern development and the beginning of the renewal of Jewish settlement in the country. Most of the Arab population in the north was residing in the interior of Galilee, usually in small villages, and was only able to scrape a bare living from the inhospitable mountain environment. A small number of Jewish families lived in some of the Arab villages, claiming a long tradition of settlement there. Most of the villages in Galilee were composed then — and still are — of one religious group, Muslim, Christian or Druze. The Druze uphold a religion that evolved from Islam in the Middle Ages and are found mainly in southern Syria, Lebanon and northern Israel. Only a few of the villages in Galilee had a mixture of several religious groups. In such villages each religious group congregated in its own section or neighborhood. Such segregation is still present to a large extent within these religiously mixed villages and in mixed towns that grew out of such villages. In the mid-nineteenth century there were four small ancient towns—Tiberias, Zefat, Nazareth and Acre—on the skirts of the Galilee mountains. They served as commercial centers to their respective village neighbors. The first three commanded important religious positions: Tiberias and Zefat for Jews and Nazareth for Christians. Tiberias, on the Sea of Galilee, and Zefat, high on the mountains of eastern Galilee, were shared by Arabs and Jews, each group clinging to its own quarter of town. Nazareth, no more than the size of a village, was inhabited by Arabs, many of them Christians who aspired to keep the ancient sites holy to Christianity. Acre too was by then an Arab town that owed its existence to its ancient maritime role on the eastern Mediterranean coast.

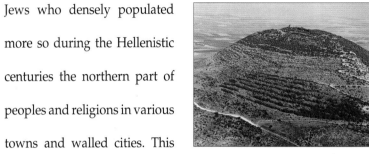

Mount Tabor in the 1930s. A winding road was cut on its slopes to allow access to the new church built at the top.

Since the middle of the nineteenth century, as the country opened up to European influence and as Jewish immigration increased, many changes have taken place in this region, which had formerly maintained a rather stable population. In Nazareth, situated in a small valley, many new Christian churches and pilgrim hospices were built in the vicinity of the holy Christian sites. A modern town grew around these churches, prospering on the commerce generated by the growing numbers of pilgrims and tourists. With time, the town climbed the slopes, gradually incorporating the few

Above: Nazareth is a city of churches and mosques.

Below: Kibbutz Mishmar Ha'emeq in the Jezreel valley, at the foot of the Menashe hills, in 1933.

Christian monasteries that had been built along with the new churches. At the end of the nineteenth century, Nazareth was linked to the coast by a carriageway, giving the town a head start in commerce and helping to turn it into a central market for its surroundings. However, unlike Jaffa, Jews did not come to settle in Nazareth. Neither did Acre attract the new Jewish immigrants, who continued to prefer the ancient Jewish urban centers in the region — Zefat and Tiberias. As the main destinations of the Jewish settlers were Jerusalem and later Jaffa, the Galilean towns remained behind in terms of modern development, a fact that underlies the present status of the north as a peripheral region of Israel.

Only in the beginning of the twentieth century, a few decades later than in the Jerusalem area and along the coastal plain, did the northern region undergo substantial changes. Walled towns spread beyond their confines and new neighborhoods were built to accommodate the growing number of inhabitants aspiring for better and more modern housing. Modern roads were constructed to facilitate commerce and tourism. It was toward the end of the nineteenth century that Jewish settlement commenced, with the establishment of a series of new *moshavot*, mostly on the eastern edge of Galilee. Later on, cooperative Jewish rural settlements—

kibbutzim and *moshavim* — were introduced to the valleys surrounding the mountains of Galilee, the first ones settling in the Jordan valley south of the Sea of Galilee in the 1910s. As Jewish agricultural settlement efforts gradually intensified in the 1920s and 1930s, the valleys south and west of the Galilee mountains also witnessed a spread of Jewish cooperative villages, which cultivated its formerly swampy areas, making it one of the most productive regions in the country.

Once the State of Israel was formed in 1948 and was in a position to pursue a policy of increasing Jewish settlement in areas where it had barely been present, additional cooperative Jewish rural settlements were established across the north, in the mountains and valleys alike. Concomitantly, a series of new Jewish towns was founded in several sections of the north, primarily housing new immigrants. In more recent decades, small suburban and exurban Jewish communities have been established across the interior parts of Galilee. For years, the landscape in these regions of Galilee had been characterized by the presence of Arab villages. Now they have been joined by many new Jewish settlements casting their own distinct character on the landscape. At the same time, some of the Arab villages have developed in size and in architectural style, gradually joining the trend of urbanization, particularly in the western parts of Galilee.

Ancient-New Towns The landscape changes in the ancient towns of Galilee are most exciting to follow because one can look at photographs that were taken in them even as early as the 1850s and 1860s. In those days the towns preserved a landscape carried over from far in the past. Nowadays, the ancient part of town is but a quarter in the commercial section of a modern and developing city.

A view of Tiberias from the south in 1937. The town spread west of the Sea of Galilee on the mountain slope.

Tiberias Tiberias (Teveria in Hebrew) did not witness expansion beyond its walls until the beginning of the twentieth century, a late development in comparison with Jerusalem and Jaffa. With the expansion, new streets were added beyond the walls, which had been severely damaged in an earthquake in 1837. Later, new neighborhoods were built along the roads leading to the city and in the 1920s, the city began climbing the steep slope on the west. A modern Jewish neighborhood, named Qiryat Shemuel, was built on a terrace hanging about three hundred feet over the Sea of Galilee. It was yet another example of garden neighborhoods springing up next to the old parts of town. The new neighborhood attempted to adopt the main hotel and resort business that had developed along the shores of the Sea of Galilee. However, with the flight of the Arab population during the 1948 Arab-Jewish war and the subsequent clearance of much of the Old City of Tiberias, commerce and tourism returned with full force to the seashore. There, alongside the Sea of Galilee, the landscape has been transformed entirely. High-rise hotel buildings tower over some remnants of the Old City walls and a few old buildings, including a mosque. On the shore itself, fish restaurants cater to the tourists while pleasure boats ply in the waters. On top of the mountain is Upper Tiberias, a large residential area first built in the 1950s to provide housing for the many Jewish immigrants that came to settle in the city in those years. Although Upper Tiberias commands a breathtaking view of the Sea of Galilee and its environs, it has not evolved into a highly desirable place of residence. The neighborhood's original designation as an area of public housing for the recent immigrants predetermined its social composition for years to come. Thus, the urban area closer to the seashore has remained the main focus of urban life in Tiberias.

Zefat The town of Zefat (Safed) encircles a high peak in the eastern mountains of Galilee. Zefat was chosen by the medieval Crusaders as a location for one of their major fortresses and since then it has functioned as the urban center of eastern Upper Galilee. After a flourishing period during the sixteenth and seventeenth centuries, when Zefat functioned as a major Jewish economic and religious center, the city dwindled in size due to unrest and plagues in the region. It suffered a major blow in 1837, when the severe earthquake that damaged the walls of Tiberias also destroyed most of Zefat's built-up area. Many of the Jews of Zefat left for other cities in the country, mostly Jerusalem. The Arab and Jewish population of Zefat lived in separate quarters, the Jews inhabiting the north and

northwestern areas on the mountain. The Jews occupied two distinct neighborhoods. In one lived Ashkenazi Jews, originally immigrants from Eastern Europe, while the other neighborhood served the Sephardic Jews, descendants of Jews that had been expelled from Spain in 1492 and eventually settled in the town of Zefat. In the midst of a fierce battle during the 1948 Arab-Jewish war, the Arab population left the city. It was immediately settled by a large number of new Jewish immigrants, most of them inhabiting the new housing projects built around the old town, expanding the city to the east and south. The face of Zefat completely changed during those few years. It no longer clung to the peak of the mountain but spread over the neighboring hills. Nevertheless, Zefat did not lose the old town's charm. Along with Tiberias, it has emerged as a minor tourist and resort center, where the old town, its religious sites and its art studios are the main attractions. The cool summer weather in this mountainous picturesque town brings to its modest hotels people looking for a comfortable season away from the humid cities of the coastal plain.

Above: Arab neighborhoods in the eastern parts of Zefat in 1937.

Below: Nazareth in the 1930s.

Nazareth and Nazerat Illit The city of Nazareth gradually rose from its rural character in the early nineteenth century to become a thriving city that now serves as the major urban center of southern Galilee as well as a cultural and political center for the Arab population of Israel. Nazareth's modern revival, like Jerusalem's, is related to the growing interest and influence of European powers in the country at the time of the Ottoman rule. Already in the eighteenth century, the local rulers permitted reconstruction of the Christian churches that had been destroyed in the Middle

Ages after the defeat of the Crusaders by Muslim forces. The Church of Annunciation—built in antiquity at the site where according to tradition, Mary, the mother of Jesus, was told that she was to have a child, and rebuilt

by the Crusaders to be destroyed again by the Mameluks in 1263—was renewed in 1730. As more and more Christian pilgrims arrived to visit the Christian holy sites in Nazareth, more hospices and churches were erected in and around the cluster of Christian sites already existing in the oldest part of the ancient town. New residences as well as Christian monasteries and schools were built on the slopes of the mountain hanging over the city, as it was gradually climbing upward to accommodate its constant growth and development. When the British came to rule the country in 1917, the population of Nazareth was about eight thousand, two thirds of whom were Christians, making the city the capital of the Northern District, a fact that enhanced its role as an economic center in Lower Galilee. By the end of the British period, in 1947, the population of Nazareth had grown to seventeen thousand inhabitants, about nine tenths of whom were Christian Arabs. Nazareth's population growth was accelerated after 1948, with the establishment of the State of Israel. Many Arab villagers from Galilee moved to live in Nazareth, which soon became the largest Arab city in Israel. The city's population doubled in the next two decades and was close to repeating that toward the end of the twentieth century, when it was close to sixty thousand without its immediate suburbs. The most dramatic change in the landscape of the central area of Nazareth was the rise of the Church of Annunciation. It was rebuilt as a modern structure between 1955 and 1969, over the ruins of its predecessors. Its high dome stands out over

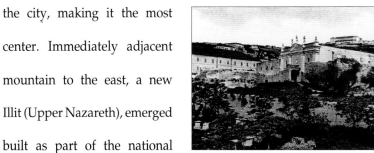

The Church of Annunciation in Nazareth before its renovation and the addition to it of an enormous dome.

the city, making it the most prominent building in the city center. Immediately adjacent to Arab Nazareth, on the mountain to the east, a new Jewish town, called Nazerat Illit (Upper Nazareth), emerged in 1957. The new town was built as part of the national policy to establish new towns in the peripheral regions of the country. Nazerat Illit was settled by a large number of Jewish immigrants, and continues to be populated with every new wave of Jewish immigration. Recently, the city has spread to the north and east, over the crests of the ridges surrounding Nazareth, dramatically transforming the mountainous landscape. As local Jewish residents moved to the newer housing, Arab families from Nazareth moved into the neighboring Jewish city in search of improved dwelling. Gradually, the new city has become home to a sizable Arab population. Together, Nazareth and Nazerat Illit now form the core of a nascent metropolitan region in what had been mostly rural landscape until just a few decades ago.

Acre Acre (Akko in Hebrew), a coastal city that has had ups and downs since antiquity, was destroyed in 1291 by the Muslim Mameluks, when they defeated the Crusaders there. In the mid-eighteenth century,

Acre was rebuilt as a magnificent walled city by a local Galilean ruler. Its fortifications, aided by cannons, were strong enough to withstand the siege by Napoleon Bonaparte on his military expedition to the Levant in 1799. But it soon lost its primacy in the region as a port to Beirut and Haifa, deep water ports that were able to handle the modern ocean-going steam boats, which the shallow waters of Acre could not do. At the turn of the twentieth century, Acre started to emerge from within its walls. A new quarter was built north of the city, in an attempt to push the city into the modern era. But the competition of the new Haifa

The Old City of Acre from the sea, in the 1930s.

port, built by the British in the 1920s, dealt a big blow to Acre's economy and the city was reduced to a small market town with an insignificant fishing port. The Jews left in the city moved away to take part in the fortunes of Haifa — the prospering city across the bay to the south. At the end of the British period, only twelve thousand people lived in Acre. As was the case with other ancient towns in Galilee, the State of Israel brought with it a demographic revolution for Acre. Jewish immigrants came to settle in the half-vacant city after the Arab-Jewish war and, later, in the many housing projects built to the north and east of the old town. The built-up area of Acre has more than tripled since 1948 and its population has grown substantially. Its economy, however, did not follow suit. The city of Acre gradually integrated with other adjoining cities near Haifa to become suburbs in the large city's metropolitan region. Acre's main appeal lies in its antiquities. In recent years, many structures from the time of the Crusaders have been discovered and unearthed, such as St. John's Crypt, which was the Crusaders' refectory. The Great Mosque and the Khan el-Umdan (a huge hostel) date back to the glorious days of Acre in the second half of the eighteenth century. The Crusaders' underground structures, the Muslim edifices and the picturesque surroundings of alleys and markets, make the Old City of Acre an attraction for tourists, from Israel and abroad.

The Galilean *moshavot* During the last quarter of the nineteenth century, when the Jewish population started to build its own agricultural villages (*moshavot*) in the country, many were established in eastern Galilee. They all had to confront great odds and, to their dismay, were to find that with time they were placed in the country's periphery. The main economic and urban developments took

The main street of Yessud Hama'ala in the Hula valley in the late nineteenth century.

place in the coastal plain, mainly around the city of Tel Aviv. Unlike *moshavot* in the coastal region, which grew to become thriving cities due to their central locations, the Galilean *moshavot* remained villages, still keeping much of the old atmosphere and maintaining the old houses. It is in these present landscapes and not only in the museum or album that history can be found.

In those early years of Jewish settlement two clusters of *moshavot* were founded in eastern Galilee. Rosh Pina was one of the earliest attempts at Jewish rural settlement, made in 1878 by a group of Jews from Zefat. They, like other Jewish groups at the time, were fascinated by the idea of returning to agricultural life in their country and were prepared to undergo intense hardship to reach this goal. They were reinforced in 1882 by Jews from

Romania and Russia. In 1884, Rosh Pina was joined by Yessud Hama'ala on the shores of the Hula lake, now long gone because of a major drainage project in the 1950s. A few years later Mishmar Hayarden was founded near the Jordan river and Mahanayyim was founded nearby. On the northernmost edge of the Hula valley, on the verge of Lebanon, Metula was established in 1896. Two of

Kinneret, a Jewish moshava on the Sea of Galilee, in 1912.

these *moshavot* do not exist today. Mahanayyim was deserted by its settlers after only a few years because of economic difficulties; Mishmar Hayarden was destroyed in 1948 in the War of Independence and was never rebuilt as a *moshava*. Further south from the Hula valley, not far from Tiberias, several Jewish *moshavot* struck root in eastern Lower Galilee. As their northern counterparts, they too have remained to this day small settlements. Up on the plateau of lower eastern Galilee Yavne'el and its immediate neighbor Bet Gan were established at the turn of the twentieth century. Not far, close to Mount Tabor, Sejjera (Ilaniyya) and Kefar Tavor were founded. Down in the valley another three *moshavot* struck root: Migdal and Kinneret on the western shores of the Sea of Galilee and Menahamiyya to its south, near the Jordan river.

The only *moshava* in the north which grew to become a prosperous town is Nahariyya, established in 1934 on the Mediterranean coast by Jews arriving from Nazi Germany. The founders had contemplated building an agricultural community, as was then still common among many of the Jewish rural settlers, but with the immediate proximity of the seashore and the rise of the resort industry Nahariyya has moved along with the processes of urbanization. In the 1950s the little *moshava* grew considerably with the addition of large scale housing projects on its northern and eastern outskirts. Consequently Nahariyya ceased to be a small haven of German Jewish culture and soon became a melting pot of all kinds of immigrant groups landing in the country. Today, the central parts of urbanized Nahariyya take the shape of a tourist oriented commercial center.

Intensive Jewish Cooperative Settlement Galilee and especially the valleys around it have witnessed intensive Jewish settlement activity in the forms of *kibbutzim* and *moshavim*. The forerunners of these new kinds of Jewish settlements were indeed founded in the north of the country. The earliest *kibbutzim* (the first being Degania founded in 1909, and Kibbutz Kinneret, founded in 1913) were established just south of the Sea of Galilee, where the Jordan river continues its course to the south. Here the new form of communal life was first tried and crystallized. In the 1920s and onwards, more *kibbutzim* were founded — Degania Bet, Afiqim, Ashdot Ya'aqov, Bet Zera, Sha'ar Hagolan and Masada. In a few decades, this relatively desolate part of the country was transformed into one of its most flourishing agricultural areas. The changes that took place in the landscape are impressive. The many photographs taken of the area at different times from the nearby mountains attest to this change very evidently. Those who are accustomed to take for granted this flourishing part of the Jordan valley are usually surprised to discover that at the turn of the century very little agriculture was developed there. A similar transformation took place

in the valleys lying on the southern rim of the Galilee mountains, the Jezreel and Harod valleys. Most of the land in these valleys was purchased since the mid-1920s by the Jewish National Fund, a Zionist land development organization that has concentrated on acquiring land for Jewish agricultural settlements. By the late 1940s, the Jezreel and Harod valleys were filled with *kibbutzim* and *moshavim*. One of the earliest and best known in the Jezreel valley is Nahalal, which was arranged in the form of a circle. Its layout is indicative of the general style of Jewish agricultural settlements in the country — well planned and structured. One of the earliest *kibbutzim* in the Harod valley is En Harod, which was founded on the southern edge of the valley near the biblical Harod spring, but was soon transferred to a more suitable location on the valley's northern edge. In the 1930s, during the disturbances between Arabs, Jews and British, the network of Jewish settlement was reinforced on the eastern margins of the valleys, as well as in the Bet She'an valley which lies on the Jordan river. A series of new Jewish settlements was built in a manner known as "Tower and Stockade." The idea was to immediately provide the newly established settlements with some measure of security. Building materials for an observation tower, a stockade and residences were prepared in advance, and all were in use the day the settlement was founded. In this way, for instance, Kibbutz Nir David (Tel Amal) at the foot of the Gilboa mountains and Kibbutz Tirat Zevi near the Jordan river were established. Tirat Zevi is part of the Bet She'an valley which occupies part of the Jordan rift valley, around the biblical town of Bet She'an. The more southerly position of the Bet She'an valley made it part of the hot and semiarid strip that extends southward to the Dead Sea, along the rift valley. The traditional Arab agriculture that had been practiced in the Bet

She'an valley before 1948 was quite poor and only modern agricultural practices have been able to promise an improved economy, although the extremely hot summers continue to be problematic.

The Hula valley in the northeastern corner of the country, where several tributaries form the source of the Jordan river, was another zone of intensive Jewish settlement by *kibbutzim*, joining the few *moshavot* established there earlier. Rich with water flowing down in streams from Mount Hermon, the Hula valley soon became one of the major Jewish agricultural areas in the country. Many of the *kibbutzim* established there were placed on the rim of the valley in an effort to mark the future of Jewish settled territory in the northeast of the country. The forerunners among the *kibbutzim* in this area were Kefar Gil'adi and Ayelet Hashahar, which were established on the western edge of the Hula valley immediately after the British had taken over and the question of the boundaries of British Palestine soon arose. Later, in the 1930s and 1940s, as part of this major effort to integrate the Hula valley into the Jewish zone of settlement, a series of *kibbutzim* was established at the foot of Mount Hermon, the better known among them being Dafna and Dan. They too were built by the "Tower and Stockade" method. Kefar Szold and Lehavot Habashan followed later on the eastern margins of the valley and Misgav Am and Manara on the western margins, close to the Lebanese border. In the three decades of British rule of the country the Hula valley and its margins were transformed into another area of intensive *kibbutz* settlement, helping to turn the valley into one of the most intensively cultivated areas in the country. The emphasis on agriculture was at the root of the changing fate of the lake at the bottom of the Hula valley. In the early 1950s, great efforts were made to drain Hula lake, which used to cover a large area of the valley and was used for fishing and harvesting reeds for making mats. In those days, Israeli policy makers and the neighboring agricultural settlements were interested in enlarging the area of cultivable land in the region. By the end of a massive drainage project the lake had shrunk to a token size as a nature reserve.

Of all the valleys south and east of the Galilee mountains, the Jezreel valley in particular soon represented the spirit of Jewish settlement and was a basis for songs, music and stories that found their place in the folklore of the Zionist settlement movement. For a long time, it was referred to as The Valley (*Ha'emeq* in Hebrew) and everyone knew what this meant. The Jezreel valley was the symbol of the country's transformation into a blossoming region as the result of Jewish settlement efforts. Moreover, the fact that some small parts of the Jezreel valley had originally been covered with swamps added a heroic dimension to the early Jewish pioneering endeavors there.

West of the Galilee mountains lies the coastal plain sometimes known as the Acre valley. In this area too,

Jewish settlement efforts were started in the 1930s, joining some existing Arab villages that were mainly strung along the western foothills of Galilee. Nahariyya, mentioned earlier, lies in the midst of this area. One of the *kibbutzim* that later settled in its vicinity is Yehi'am, which is located at the foot of a former Crusader fort. For many years, however, Jewish settlements did not penetrate the interior of Galilee, where Arab villages and small towns had been long established. The first major attempt to establish a Jewish settlement further north in Galilee only took place in 1938.

A new *kibbutz*, Hanita, was set up overnight with the help of many volunteers. The event was well publicized and grew to symbolize the determination of the Jewish population in establishing a foothold in northern Galilee, near the Lebanese border. Later, more

Kibbutz Hanita was founded in northern Galilee, on the Lebanese border, in 1938.

Jewish settlements were founded on the foothills of the Galilee mountains, but the core of the region still remained without rural Jewish settlement for some years. Only in 1948, after the establishment of the State of Israel, were Jewish settlements founded over larger areas of Galilee, particularly along the northern frontier, on the Lebanese border, as part of a government policy to increase Jewish presence in this strategic strip of land. *Kibbutzim* were established in remote locations on the mountains, along with many new *moshavim*, where new immigrants found a home. But the central part of Galilee remained lacking in significant Jewish settlement for quite a long time.

New Towns in Galilee A series of new towns, largely populated by new immigrants, were established in Galilee, most of them again on the edge of the region. They too were part of the government's policy to establish new towns all over the country's periphery. Qiryat Shemona and Hazor Hagelilit in the Hula valley were founded in the northeast, Bet She'an in the southeast and Shelomi and Migdal Ha'emeq in the west. As mentioned, the town of Nazerat Illit was set up on the southern edge of the Galilee mountains. The only new towns to be founded in the interior in those years were Ma'alot-Tarshikha in Upper Galilee and Karmi'el in Lower Galilee. Built by central government planning agencies, the public housing sector had a significant impact on the architectural style of the new towns and on the socioeconomic status of their inhabitants. Although they have significantly changed the landscape in their vicinity, they sustained much economic hardship and social deprivation for many years. Recently, however, some of them have begun to evolve into attractive residential settings, as more people prefer not to reside in the large cities and opt for small-town living. Migdal Ha'emeq attracted high technology plants and its industrial region is one of the most advanced in the country. But the most important impetus to the development of the northern towns originated in the huge immigration wave from the former Soviet Union since 1989. This impact is especially noted in Karmi'el. New neighborhoods were built there to accommodate the surging housing demand from the many immigrants. As a result Karmi'el now stretches all along the valley it is situated in, running east to west in the heart of Galilee. In the mid-1960s it was quite a small town of a couple of thousand newly settled residents. It is now well beyond the thirty-five thousand mark and increasingly growing in size as more housing is being

added. In the early days of Karmi'el, Haifa and its immediate suburbs seemed far away and irrelevant for its future development. Nowadays, however, many of Karmi'el's residents commute daily to the cities of the Haifa bay. Growing Arab Villages and Towns Arab villages in Galilee have also changed considerably in recent decades. Population growth and rising

The Druze village of Beit Jan in upper Galilee in 1963.

levels of income have generated housing construction on their outskirts, transforming many of them into towns. The former village of Sakhnin in Lower Galilee is now a sizable town, serving as a commercial center for its surroundings. Likewise, the formerly small and sleepy town of Shefar'am (Shafa Amer in Arabic), shared by Muslims, Christians and Druze, now serves as a thriving commercial center for the southwestern part of Lower Galilee. It spread from the little hill it once stood on to the little valleys below. Kafr Yasif, another multi-religious town, constitutes a local center on the foothills of Upper Galilee. In recent years this once little village has grown into a sizable one by attracting migrants from other Arab villages in the region. In Galilee's interior, the large village of Rameh, not far from the new Jewish town of Karmi'el, is now expanding on the steep slope that marks the boundary between Upper and Lower Galilee. This sight of houses climbing on the slope of a mountain in search for more space for a growing population is characteristic of many Arab villages and towns in Galilee. The expansion of Arab villages in Galilee is reflected in their form and in the landscape of the region. Many of these villages are no longer tiny compact places occupying the very top of a hill or hiding at its foot. They are now spread over a large area, often being built in what were once cultivated fields and orchards. The old core of the village characterized by winding narrow alleys and outdated structures, has been discarded by many households for the modern and more spacious houses on the expanding periphery of the village. Many of the new Arab houses now resemble those built in the adjacent Jewish settlements, as construction technologies and architectural styles are easily interchanged between neighbors.

New Exurban Communities In more recent years, even the heart of Galilee has been densely settled by Jews, mostly small communities seeking to live in suburban or exurban settings. The mountains of

Galilee have proved suitable surroundings to materialize such a dream. Moreover, the Israeli government, pursuing its policy of strengthening Jewish presence in those parts of the region that had been settled by many Arab villages, encouraged this new Jewish residential trend by providing for numerous appropriate sites and generous assistance for those willing to make their homes in the rather remote new communities in the heart of the mountains. These new communities have tended to stay small in size and many are populated with middle-class households, often endeavoring to preserve the intimate character of the place and its social homogeneity. The spread of these Jewish settlements has had substantial impact on the landscape of Galilee. Mountain tops and crests, which formerly were void of human habitation, are now covered with settlements composed of large white-painted houses, with red-tiled roofs. These modern houses stand out in the landscape as very different from the traditional architecture of flat-roofed buildings common in the neighboring Arab villages. Many of the new Jewish settlements are conspicuous because they have been placed on high ground — on the top of mountains or on their upper slopes where land was free of Arab villages, usually found near the bottom of the valleys so as to be close to cultivable land. They are therefore conspicuous from many places in the region. Wide areas of mountains can be observed from the settlements themselves and indeed many of them have come to be known as 'observatories' (*mitzpim* in Hebrew).

The new exurban Jewish settlement of Zurit, southwest of Karmiel, in 1997.

Tiberias lies on the western shores of the Sea of Galilee. For centuries it was enclosed behind walls. In a photograph from 1875 the town was still behind its aged walls.
Outside the city walls there were just a few building lying in the midst of rocky fields.

By the end of the twentieth century Tiberias is much larger in size than it was in the beginning of the modern era.
The walls were dismantled; new neighborhoods were built on the lower slope of the nearby mountain hanging over the town from the west.
Most of the buildings in the old town were replaced by new hotels and commercial building towering over the Sea of Galilee.

Hot springs, located about a mile and a half south of Tiberias and seen in the foreground of the photograph from the turn of the twentieth century, made the town a popular spa years ago. They were an early base for the development of resort tourism in the town.
Modest hostels and boarding houses used to provide accommodation for the spa's clientele.

Opposite: Nowadays large modern hotels, one of them built between the city and the spa, have taken over from the hostels and the boarding houses. A newly-widened modern highway provides easy access to the city and its tourist attractions. On the once rocky beach, parks and camping grounds were prepared for vacationers.

Zefat (or Safed) clings to the upper slopes of a high mountain in eastern Galilee. Jews and Arabs lived there side by side for ages. The Jewish quarter is seen further out in the photograph taken in 1912.

Opposite: Zefat attracts tourists who enjoy the old architecture, the art shops and the cool summers.

The mountains around Zefat were quite barren due to the semiarid climate and the poor soils. Olive groves covered patches of land on the slopes next to a narrow and unpaved road leading out of town, where the ground was soft enough for cultivation, as seen in a picture from the 1930s.

In recent years new villa neighborhoods were built on the outskirts of Zefat town, along the roads now wide and paved with asphalt. The top of the mountains near Zefat, like many others in Galilee, are now covered with pine trees, thanks to forestation efforts made mostly by the Jewish National Fund.

Zefat viewed from the north in the 1930s. The town lay in a ring around the peak of the mountain.

Right: In 1869 Nazareth was still a small town in Lower Galilee. It mostly lay at the bottom of the valley, close to the venerated ancient Christian sites.

*Below: A view of Nazareth from the bottom of the valley towards the mountain in the northeast in the 1880s.
It was then still a small town clinging to the holy Christian sites.*

Right: Mary's Well in Nazareth in the nineteenth century.

Opposite: Nazareth climbed up the mountain to become the largest Arab city in Galilee. The most prominent addition to the new urban landscape of the city was the new edifice of the Church of Annunciation.

Top: Immediately next to the ancient city of Nazareth lies the new town of Nazerat Illit (Upper Nazareth). It was founded in 1957 on the rocky mountain crest east of Nazareth, facing Mount Tabor, and was settled largely by new Jewish immigrants. The 1958 picture shows the beginning of construction of a new housing project.

Opposite Top: In the late 1990s Nazerat Illit is spread over the mountain crest facing Mount Tabor.

Bottom: In 1954 the area where Nazerat Illit lies today still lacked significant urban development. Nazareth lies to the left of the photograph.

Opposite Bottom: Nazerat Illit is now a fairly large city. Additional new housing was built in the 1990s, in response to the growth of its population brought about by the large wave of Jewish immigration from the former Soviet Union.

Above: Acre is an ancient port town on the Mediterranean coast of Galilee. Until the 1920s camels were an important means of transportation between Acre and Haifa to the south.

Opposite: Old Acre maintains its ancient character, attracting many visitors who come to admire its markets, fortresses, mosques and Crusaders' edifices. The old fishermen's port is another attraction.

Much effort was devoted to unveil the ancient beauty of old Acre. Old buildings were excavated and reconstructed. Part of these efforts was the cleaning of the moats outside the city walls that during previous years were filled with refuse and earth.

Above: Acre is now composed of two parts. The Old City lies on a promontory into the Mediterreanean Sea. The new part is spread to the north and the east.

Left: Most of Acre in the early 1920s was enclosed behind the walls of the Old City. Its new part (on the right) was still only in its initial stage.

Above: Rosh Pina was founded in 1878 as the first Jewish moshava in eastern Galilee, on the western margins of the Hula valley. Around 1910, when this picture was taken, Rosh Pina, after about three decades of existence, was still a small village with no paved streets.

Left: At the end of the twentieth century, Rosh Pina, though it has not grown to become a large city as many of its counterparts on the coastal plain near Tel Aviv-Yafo, is now well furnished with paved roads and other modern urban facilities. This makes it an attractive residential option for those who wish to live in a comfortable rustic setting.

Above: Metula is the northernmost moshava in the country, founded in 1896 on what later became the boundary with Lebanon. Dairy produce was an important component in the economy of the village.

Right: With time new streets were added to Metula, and after many years of total dependence on farming there is now a thriving tourist and resort economy which is occasionally hurt when the border area is subject to hostilities.

Top: Afula was established in 1925 with a dream to be the central city of the Jezreel valley. Many people, guided by this dream, bought properties in Afula. In a picture of 1928 the place is full of construction activity, including the erection of a new domed synagogue. But the thrust of urban development went to the coastal cities.
Afula remained a small urban settlement for many years, a symbol of a broken dream in a country where dreams came true so often.

Above: Afula today is a sizable town serving as a center for the Jezreel valley.

Left: The railroad station in Afula in the 1930s from where one could travel by train to Haifa or Damascus. A few years later the railroad crossing the Jezreel valley was dismantled.

Above: Nahariyya at the end of the twentieth century lost almost all its original character as an agricultural community. It is one of the main cities in the north of the country, with resort tourism and industry serving as the main basis of the local economy.

Right: Nahariyya, two years after its founding as an agricultural settlement in 1934, was still a small village on the Mediterranean coast. It is located not far from the Lebanese border, running along the top of the mountain ridge seen in the far distance in the photograph. Like many other Jewish settlements in those days, Nahariyya stood out amidst its surrounding landscape by its tall water tower.

Above: Kevuzat Degania, later known as Degania Alef, was the first Jewish cooperative settlement in the Jordan valley immediately south of the Sea of Galilee. It started in 1909 as a farm managed by the Zionist Organization. In 1910 the farm was handed over to the workers to set up a communal village, the first kibbutz in the country. A new wooden house was built to serve as the first modern structure in Degania Alef.

Right: In 1914 Degania Alef consisted of a few new farm buildings.

Farm Dganiah

Top: Degania Alef is located where the Jordan river leaves the Sea of Galilee. In its early days the river was not yet spanned by a bridge.

Bottom: The Jordan river near Degania Alef in 1997.

Top: In 1917 Degania Alef was already surrounded by orchards but still a small settlement striving to transform this once quite desolate region into an agriculturally productive area.

Bottom: Sixty years later the original farm area is part of a pleasant environment of the now large settlement of Degania Alef.

Top: The Jordan valley south of the Sea of Galilee was already a thriving region in 1948. In the foreground is Kevuzat Kinneret, one of the kibbutzim established in the region following Degania Alef. Degania Alef itself lies further away near the lake.

Bottom: In 1997 the Jordan valley is contiguously settled by kibbutzim.

Right: Degania Alef near the Sea of Galilee in 1997.

Top: Kibbutz Merhavia was the first Jewish settlement established in 1910 in the Jezreel valley at the foot of Giv'at Hamoreh. It started as an agricultural farm run by the Zionist Organization and later was turned into a kibbutz. The picture shows Kibbutz Merhavia in its early years.

Bottom: The old farm compound in Kibbutz Merhavia in 1946.

Opposite: Kibbutz Merhavia nowadays is a flourishing settlement close to the town of Afula. The mountain of Giv'at Hamoreh stand in the background. The old farm compound is still around.

Top: En Harod was first established in 1921 as a kibbutz on the southern side
of the Harod valley, near the Harod spring at the foot of Mount Gilboa.

Bottom: In 1925 there was an En Harod railroad station near the new settlement.
The station and the railroad are long gone.

Above: En Harod was moved to the northern side of the Harod valley in 1931.
The foothills of Mount Gilboa are in the far background.

Left: Nowadays En Harod consists of two prospering kibbutzim, each with its own political affiliation. The split occurred in 1951 as a result of a political rift.

Top Right: Nahalal was the first moshav to be established in the country. It was founded in 1921 in the Jezreel valley. Apart from tents, the first structures were made of corrugated iron.

Top Left: Farm houses were built a few years later along the circular street that made Nahalal famous around the world.

Bottom Right: Preparing stones for the paving of the newly planned road to Nahalal in 1924.

Bottom Left: The first mailman in Nahalal.

Opposite: The circular shape of Nahalal endures, although everything else – people, organizational structure and architecture – has changed.

Kibbutz Nir David (also known as Tel Amal) was established in 1936 at the foot of Mount Gilboa. It is considered the first Jewish settlement to be built in those years in the "Tower and Stockade" design.

Above: Nir David in 1997.

Left: Today the old site of the "Tower and Stockade" settlement is reconstructed as a museum in the midst of present day Nir David.

Above: Tel Hai is one of the national symbols of early Zionist history. In 1920 eight of the settlers defending it, headed by Yosef Trumpeldor, fell in a skirmish between Jews and Arabs at a time when the territorial fate of the water-rich Hula valley within the realm of the British Mandate in Palestine was at stake.

Left: As often happens to revered places, Tel Hai too has remained almost the same as it had been in 1920 and was turned into a museum. But its former surroundings have changed. Jewish settlements have filled the Hula valley, including the nearby town of Qiryat Shemona.

Above: The "Tower and Stock-ade" design was used in the construction of Dafna, a kibbutz established in 1939 on the north-eastern edge of Hula valley, at the foot of Mount Hermon.

Right: Dafna nowadays is far away from its early beginnings.

Opposite Top: During the 1950s a large project to drain Lake Hula was undertaken with a view to reclaiming land for agriculture. Only a small body of water remained in the far southern tip of the former lake to serve as a nature reserve.

Opposite Bottom: In the early 1950s a large part of the Hula valley was still covered by the waters of Lake Hula.

Top: The area of the drained Hula lake that used to extend close to the houses of Kibbutz Hulata was taken over with agricultural cultivation.

Center: Fishing boats and fishing nets in 1946 at Sede Nehemia, a kibbutz on what was then the Hula lake. All this area of the lake is presently under cultivation.

Bottom: Harvesting cane in 1946 in the Hula lake near Hulata, a kibbutz that was established on the shores of the lake with a view to build a lake-oriented economy. This economic base vanished with the draining of the lake.

Opposite Top: The establishment of Kibbutz Hanita in western Upper Galilee, on the Lebanese border, in 1938, symbolized Jewish determination to extend Jewish settlements into areas where Jewish presence had not existed.

Opposite Bottom: Hanita is now a large kibbutz surrounded by other Jewish settlements.

From Top to Bottom:
Many volunteers from around the country joined in the efforts to build a settlement in only one day so it would be able to defend itself at the end of the day.

Volunteers carrying construction materials to the new site of Kibbutz Hanita.

Building the barbed wire fence around Kibbutz Hanita on the day of its founding.

A view from the tower on the compound of Hanita as it was being constructed in 1938. Note the wooden frame filled with gravel and sand that was used as the stockade.

Top: A view of Ya'ara in 1954. Ya'ara was established as an immigrant moshav in 1950 near a border police station dating from the 1930s. Much hardship confronted the early settlers.

Bottom: Clearing rocks to reclaim land for agriculture in Ya'ara in 1950.

Opposite: Ya'ara today. Beduin veterans have joined the Jewish inhabitants to form a mountain community in northwestern Galilee.

Top: Qiryat Shemona in 1959 was a new town housing several thousands of newly arrived immigrants. The town was founded in the northwestern end of the Hula valley, at the foot of Upper Galilee mountains and facing Mount Hermon and the Golan Heights.

Center: As in other new immigrant towns, houses built in the early years were very small and modest. Each house contained two dwelling units, each consisting of only one or one and a half rooms, with a small lot outside. Those provided with this kind of housing were considered the lucky ones. Others spent some years in temporary structures made of materials such as wood or corrugated iron.

Bottom: The makeshift ''shopping center'' in Qiryat Shemona in the early 1950s serving immigrants from many cultures.

Opposite Top: More than half a century later, Qiryat Shemona is a town of twenty thousand inhabitants. The original houses, so small in early years, have grown into spacious homes. Middle-rise apartment buildings were recently built in the center of the town lending it an urban image, that had been missing in prior decades.

Opposite Bottom: At the end of the twentieth century Qiryat Shemona looks like any other town in Israel. It too has the now ubiquitous villas and cottages as well as the tall residential buildings. It has parks and play grounds, shopping centers and commercial buildings. It too has wide, well paved streets flanked by sidewalks.

Top: November 1963 – just before the cornerstone of the new town of Karmi'el was laid in mountainous Galilee. In the far distance, on the lower slope, is the Arab village of Rame. The Jewish moshav of Shazor sits at the bottom of the Bet kerem valley. Karmi'el was built as part of a policy to increase Jewish presence in the core of Galilee.

Bottom: February 1997 – thirty three years after founding day Karmi'el stands as a town of thirty-five thousand inhabitants. A large part of the Bet kerem valley is now occupied by Karmi'el's new neighborhoods, some of them built to accommodate the large wave of Jewish immigration from the former Soviet Union in the early 1990s.

Top: Rame, an Arab village on the border between Upper and Lower Galilee, in the 1950s. The village lies on the main road between Acre and Zefat and has a mixed population of Christians, Druze and Muslims. Olive groves were still important in the economy of the village.

Bottom: Rame has gradually grown along the slopes of the mountains rising over the Bet kerem valley.

Top: In 1949 the Arab town of Shefar'am (Shafa Amer in Arabic) in western Lower Galilee was no more than a large village. It was still mostly confined to the top of its hill. The population of the town consists of Muslims, Christians and Druze.

Bottom: Half a century later, Shefar'am, a town of twenty five thousand is spread over a large area, far beyond its original core. Its new neighborhoods were built according to the more modern construction methods and style and present a drastic change from the way the old ones were built in the past.

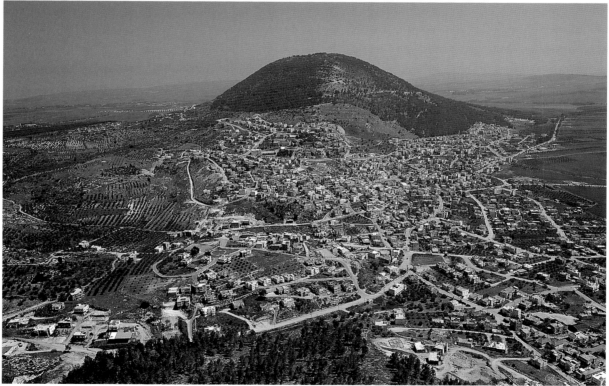

Top: Dabburiyye, a small Muslim Arab village at the foot of Mount Tabor in the late 1930s.

Bottom: Dabburiyye in the late 1990s extends over a wide area at the foot of
Mount Tabor. Like many Arab villages in Galilee, Dabburiyye experienced very
little migration, resulting in much local housing construction.

Israel's South: The Negev

The southern part of Israel, known in Hebrew as the Negev, occupies more than half of the country. However, with a semiarid climate in its northern regions and an arid climate to the south, it is the least inhabited section of Israel. For ages, before the beginning of Jewish settlement, the Negev was only sparsely occupied by Beduin Arabs, who made a living from agriculture. Only in antiquity, and Byzantine periods, was the merchant towns commanding Arabia and the Mediterranean

Beersheba in 1907, seven years after its establishment, was still a small desert town in the northern Negev.

herding, trade and intermittent especially during the Roman Negev settled with flourishing the trade routes between coast. The reconstructed ancient town of Avdat, which had operated a strategic caravan route, is an outstanding example of the sizable Nabatean and Byzantine towns that had once dotted the arid Negev but later succumbed to the vicissitudes of history.

Beersheba — The Negev Center The turn of the twentieth century marked the beginning of change in the Negev. In 1900, the Ottoman rulers, striving to improve their control over the restless Beduins and to bring a touch of modernity to the Negev, established the modern town of Beersheba as the region's focal point. Its streets were laid out in a gridiron design—as many modern towns are—but its houses and markets kept the look of a small, old, Middle Eastern town. This style was maintained under the British, when they took over the country from the Ottoman Turks in 1917. It was only with the establishment of the State of Israel that Beersheba, and with it other places in the Negev, underwent substantial changes. The town was left by its Arab inhabitants as the result of the war in 1948 and was then settled by a large number of Jews, many of them new immigrants, who first found a place of residence in the vacant houses and later in the new housing projects of the newly expanding city. The new residential areas were mainly built to the northeast. The "old town" of Beersheba is now but a small area of the contemporary city, although it still functions as its commercial center and is still the site of the traditional markets that bring together Arabs and Jews from the region and attract the occasional tourist from abroad. The city is now one of the largest in Israel, serving as the capital of the Negev and its main economic center. In recent decades, many Jewish immigrants from the former Soviet Union have settled in Beersheba, contributing to the cultural flavor of the city, especially the arts, and to its economy. As a result of this massive immigration new neighborhoods have been built, expanding the city into the desert.

Around Beersheba and across the south of Israel, a series of less spectacular yet substantial changes also took place in the last decades, most of them in the northern sections of the region. One of these changes was the establishment of a group of new towns in the 1950s, when the State of Israel embarked on an ambitious policy of building new towns in the peripheral regions in the north and

south of the country. Among the southern towns are Ofakim, Arad, Dimona, Yeruham and Mitzpe Ramon. With the exception of Ofakim, which was established as an agricultural town, these new towns were designed to serve as urban bases for the industrial extraction of raw materials, which are abundant in the region. The nearby Dead Sea is rich in minerals, such as potassium and bromide, used in agriculture and industry, and the northeastern Negev is abundant in phosphates for agriculture. In addition to the the mineral-based industries other kinds of factories were encouraged by the Israeli governments to operate in the new towns in the Negev, many in the textile industry, in order to provide a livelihood to their inhabitants. In a way, the particular urban style

of settlement has retained the character of the ancient days, when the Negev was dotted with trading towns on caravan routes. Although nowadays the economic base has changed to mineral extraction and a wider variety of mineral-based industries, the common denominator of the distant past and the contemporary reality is the urban character of human settlement. The lack of vast agricultural areas in this arid region underlies the primarily urban nature of localities, when intensive settlement and development does indeed occur in it.

Above Top: The new town of Dimona in the Negev in 1960.

Above Bottom: The new town of Arad in the Negev in 1960.

Left: The Dead Sea Works in 1967.

The Dead Sea minerals attracted modern development already in the 1930s, when the Dead Sea Works were established, first at the northern end of the sea and later at its southern tip, near Mount Sodom, where extraction of potassium and bromide products are currently taking place. The entire southern section of the Dead Sea, within Israeli territory, has been transformed into a huge salt pan, where the enriched salt water evaporates and is then drawn to the extraction plants on the shores of the Dead Sea. The shore area, formerly desolate and dry, now looks like a sizable industrial town, only without residential neighborhoods. These are located in the nearby towns on the Negev mountains, such as Dimona and Arad. The landscape along the western shores of the Dead Sea, not far from the Dead Sea Works, is also changing. A strip of hotels and spas has recently sprung up to accommodate demand for the health related qualities of the sea's waters and the mineral springs. What was recently a rather desolate shoreline is now teeming with visitors and tourists enjoying the spas and breathtaking views of the lowest place on earth — some 1,300 feet below sea level. The visitors are also attracted to the formidable mountain of Masada, which hangs over the Dead Sea to the west and tells a thrilling story of a Roman siege and Jewish heroism in antiquity. Following the end of the Jewish war against the Roman occupation in 70 A.D., a group of Jewish rebels took refuge on the top of the mountain, where King Herod had built his palace two centuries earlier. The story of the Roman siege around Masada and its tragic end, when the occupants took their own lives rather than go into captivity, has been told to posterity by the writings of Josephus Flavius, a politician and historian of the time. The archeological setting of the story was unearthed in the 1960s by a massive excavation. From a lonely mountain hiding its story for ages, Masada has turned into a major tourist attraction, where many climb the high cliffs by foot or cable car to wonder at the standing remains and the saga that accompanies them.

Raising the Israeli flag in Umm Rashrash as it became Elat on 10 March 1949.

Elat and the Arava A percentage of the minerals extracted in the Negev and from the Dead Sea finds its way southward to Elat, a port city on the Gulf of Elat (or Aqaba) that opens to the Red Sea and the Indian Ocean. From there, the mineral products are shipped to south and east Asia. But it is not so much the port activities of Elat that marked the transformation of this tiny hamlet to a coastal town known around Europe as a major resort. Within several decades, with the surge of coastal tourism among Europeans, Elat has witnessed a significant shift — from a small settlement established after 1948, as part of the effort to cover the Negev with a series of new towns, to a major resort center in Israel. New hotels have been built along its short coastal strip and along a lagoon dug inland to provide for a larger waterfront area. Elat of today, widely expanded along the coast of the Red Sea and inland, at the foot of granite mountains, is a far cry from the desolate place it had been not so long ago. Lying between the Dead Sea and the Gulf of Elat is the Arava valley, part of the region's major rift valley (which also includes the Jordan valley). The Arava valley lies well within Israel's arid zone and has been a desolate region, almost void of human settlement, for centuries. Modern water drilling and irrigation techniques, including drip irrigation, along with sophisticated agricultural know-how, have enabled the development of a series of agricultural settlements which have not only overcome the aridity and high temperatures of the region, but have also turned them to their advantage.

The Arava region is renowned for its out-of-season vegetables and fruits, which command high prices in the markets, especially of Europe. The green fields and gardens of the Arava settlements are as prominent in their surroundings as their products are when they arrive in the marketplaces during the cold winters of Europe.

Agricultural Settlement in the Northern Negev Agriculture has also transformed the landscape of the northwestern Negev. North and northwest of Beersheba is a vast area which, prior to 1948,

was mostly settled by a sparse population of Beduin Arabs as well as a few sedentary Arab hamlets, struggling to earn a living from dry farming and herding. The advent of the State of Israel brought substantial changes to the area. The hamlets have disappeared and the remaining Beduins have been resettled in the northeastern part of the Negev, in between the towns of Beersheba, Arad and Dimona. In the early 1950s new Jewish agricultural settlements were founded in this part of the Negev. Their agricultural activity in this semiarid area was made possible by a major water conduit that carried water from the center of the country. Most of these villages were *moshavim* settled by new Jewish immigrants, many of them coming from North African

and Middle Eastern countries. The massive settlement efforts, based largely on the extension of water, has pushed the line of agricultural settlements further south, into semiarid parts of the country, where hardly any permanent agriculture was present before. Traveling through the northern Negev today, *moshavim* and *kibbutzim* surrounded by fields and orchards continually catch the eye. Before 1948, the view was quite different. Only a few Jewish settlements, all of them *kibbutzim*, had attempted to penetrate this hostile area, where rainfall is scarce and drought quite frequent. There was a need for the strong will and audacity of pioneers to overcome

these difficulties and withstand the odds. Nowadays, these initial, ground-breaking settlements are part of a dense network of Jewish villages covering the northern Negev, and are barely discernible among them. It is only the historical record that sets them apart as the pre-State early birds. The changes that took place since then in

the landscape of the early *kibbutzim* in the Negev are amazing. Places like Revivim, Mash'abe Sadeh, Urim and Gevulot, started as tiny spots in the landscape. They consisted of a few houses, keeping together as a stronghold, in a sea of sand or rock. In their early days they were known as 'observatories' (*mitzpim*) or 'points' (*nequdot*).

Above Top: Kibbutz Gevulot in the northwestern Negev in 1945 was still an experimental station in desert agriculture.

Above Bottom: The beginning of Kibbutz Revivim in the Negev in 1943.

Left: Kibbutz Shuval in the northern Negev in 1946 is one of the 11 Jewish settlements established overnight in 1946.

The northeastern section of the Negev, between Beersheba and the town of Arad, is currently densely settled by Beduin Arabs. Characteristic of their ancient way of life, they used to live dispersed over the whole area in traditional tent encampments comprising extended families or clans. This pattern took up a lot of precious space and ran against the grain of modern service provision. The Israeli government therefore initiated a policy of urbanization in the 1970s, whereby the Beduins of the region were encouraged to congregate in new towns of their own, where they would be able to build their own houses and where social services could be provided in urban settings. This would render them more sedentary and concentrated. Almost half of the Negev's Beduin population now resides in these new towns, the largest of which is Rahat, north of Beersheba. However, the sight of a Beduin town in the Negev, which is very different from the earlier small encampment of tents and shacks, is not new to the Negev. Beersheba itself, when it was built in 1900, was such a sight, as it provided urban residence for the few Beduins who opted for a change in their mode of life. Nowadays, urban landscape has become an integral part of Beduin life. The tent has given way to the house; the desert path

Beduin herds in Beersheba in the late 1920s.

A Beduin shepherd and his herd of sheep near the town of Arad in 1962.

to the urban street; the camel and herd of sheep to the car, truck and workshop in the backyard. Although Rahat and the other Beduin towns still have a long way to go to catch up with the level of development and modernity existing in the neighboring Jewish towns in the region, they have reached far from the traditional Beduin settlements that had typified the Negev in earlier times. Even the traditionally dispersed Beduin settings that have been maintained are undergoing change. Wherever building permits could be obtained, the Beduins have set aside their tents and moved into fixed structures. Only corrugated iron, wood and asbestos were common building materials a few decades ago. Nowadays, more houses are built of concrete and mortar. The black tents have given way to whitewashed houses; but the dispersed pattern is still present. All over the northeastern area of the Negev, a new quasi-modern residential landscape is unfolding, perhaps slightly disappointing the romantic tourist in search of the traditional views of the past. Here and there a tent still adjoins a newly constructed house in a Beduin place. It might provide shelter to the elderly parents who prefer to continue their old way of life. It might serve as a traditional "guest room" in times of festivity.

But, in general, the present standards of living among the Beduins are no longer what they used to be. Despite the many changes that have taken place in the Negev in the past decades, most of it is still in its natural state. It remains a sparsely populated region, the changes being concentrated in the towns and villages that were added to it by human endeavor. The broad clearings of stony plateaus still stand. Its bold mountains can still be seen in every direction, especially in its eastern and southern sections. Its ephemeral floods, which occur after sudden rain storms, still cover large expanses of valley floor for a few hours, and then disappear as if they were never there. Only the colorful blanket of flowers, quickly making use of the rich water supply, acts as a short reminder of the stormy event but

soon falls victim to the scorching sun. The blossoming desert returns to what it used to be — a barren landscape. The burial place of David Ben-Gurion, the first prime minister of the State of Israel, whose dream was to make the Negev bloom with Jewish settlement, is indicative of both the dream and the victory of the desert. Located in Sede Boker, a Jewish settlement in the middle of the Negev, Ben-Gurion's tomb faces magnificent views of "wasteland," where nature still gloriously presides. It is in Beersheba where most things happen in the Negev and, as such, the once tiny desert town is on its way to becoming Israel's fourth metropolis, alongside its older sisters: Jerusalem, Tel Aviv-Yafo and Haifa. Beersheba, originally established to perform as a focus for the Negev, maintains this role enthusiastically and with ever increasing efforts. As such, it provides a meeting place for all walks of life in the Negev: Jews, Beduin Arabs, visitors and tourists.

Above: The old part of Beersheba in 1954.

Below: The old part of Beersheba still serves as the main commercial center of the city in 1997.

*From Top to Bottom:
A general view of Beersheba in 1916, during the
First World War.*

*An aerial view of Beersheba in the 1930s. Running
from left to right in the foreground is Hebron Road.
Behind it is the Muslim cemetery. The main mosque
of the town is located in the upper left corner.*

*Many of the new immigrants arriving in the town in
the early 1950s had to temporarily reside in a tent
camp. Such a camp was known throughout Israel in
those days as a "ma'abara."*

*A 1954 view of the first housing project outside the
old town of Beersheba.*

*Opposite: An aerial view of Beersheba in 1997.
High-rise residential buildings have been recently
built in Beersheba, giving it the look of a large city.*

Top: Revivim was the first Jewish settlement to be established deep in the arid Negev in 1943. In its early days it served as an experimental station for desert agriculture. Note the meteorological post near the plowed field.

Bottom: Revivim in 1997 is a sizable kibbutz surrounded by green areas of agricultural cultivation.

*Top: Kibbutz Urim in the northern Negev in 1946, the year it
was founded. Two members of Urim are caring for young
plants growing in the sandy soil.*

*Bottom: Urim in 1997 is a green island amidst an arid
environment, thanks to water brought all the way from the
north of the country.*

Top: Kibbutz Shuval in the northern Negev in 1951, next to the al-Huzzail Beduin encampment. Shuval was established in 1946, on the night following Yom Kippur, as part of a massive operation to found eleven new Jewish settlements, including Urim, in the northern Negev.

Bottom: Kibbutz Shuval in 1997 is a well groomed settlement.

Opposite: Rahat, a new Beduin town near Kibbutz Shuval in the northern Negev in 1997. Rahat was established in the 1970s as part of a government policy to urbanize the highly dispersed Beduin population. Several other such Beduin towns have been established since.

Above: Moshav Patish, an immigrant settlement in the northwestern Negev, in 1955. The early 1950s were marked by massive settlement of new immigrant moshavim around the country, including the northwestern Negev. The first settlers of Patish, founded in 1950, came from Kurdistan.

Left: Moshav Patish in 1997. Houses have grown larger with gardens around them.

Above: Moshav Pa'amei Tashaz in the northern Negev near Kibbutz Shuval in 1954. It was one of a string of immigrant moshavim established along the road running west of Kibbutz Shuval. These settlements were known for a while as the "Shuvalim" (plural of Shuval in Hebrew), each marked by a number. Pa'amei Tashaz was known as Shuval One. It was established in 1953 by immigrants from Persia.

Right: Moshav Pa'amei Tashaz in 1997 is still trying hard to make ends meet.

Right: A general aerial view of Dimona in 1997. By now Dimona is a town of about thirty-five thousand inhabitants. It is spread over the desert in several neighborhoods, some of which have only recently been built.

Below: A view of Dimona in 1956. Dimona was then a one year-old town in the northeastern Negev, not far from the Dead Sea. It was founded as part of a government policy to establish new towns in the peripheral regions of the country. The neighboring towns of Yeruham, Mitzpe Ramon and Arad were also part of this effort. Most of the new settlers were immigrants from North Africa, mostly from Morocco. Beduin encampments were scattered nearby.

Center: The first houses in Dimona were built of local stones.

Bottom: Temporary wooden huts were built for some of the first settlers in Dimona. Young children and their teachers are seen in a photograph of 1955.

Above: Intiating the new site of the Dead Sea Works at the southern end of the Dead Sea in 1949. In 1948 the plant at the northern end of the sea was evacuated due to war circumstances. The Dead Sea is to the right; Mount Sodom to the left.

Opposite: The new magnesium plant is part of the industrial complex of the Dead Sea Works, extracting minerals from the sea and shipping its products, including fertilizers, to many parts of the world. Workers reside in neighboring towns in the northern Negev.

Above: A 1963 view of the ongoing archaeological excavations in Herod's palace at the northern end of Masada, close to the western shores of the Dead Sea.

Opposite: A view of Herod's palace in Masada after the reconstruction activities that followed the archaeological excavations. Such excavations and restoration efforts also take their share in transforming the country's landscape.

Top: Kibbutz En Gedi by the Dead Sea in 1956. In its early years, agriculture was the main endeavor in En Gedi.

Bottom: Kibbutz En Gedi in 1997. Tourist facilities and a spa are important elements in the current economy of this settlement.

Left: A sail boat on the Dead Sea in the late nineteenth century.

Top: A view of the town of Elat in its early years (early 1950s). The photograph was taken from the mountains west of the town. The Gulf of Elat is to the right. In the far background is the Jordanian town of Aqaba and the mountains above it. To the left (north) is the Arava valley extending all the way to the Dead Sea.

Bottom: A view of the town of Elat from the west in 1997. The town now has over thirty-five thousand inhabitants.

Opposite: Elat is now mostly a tourist-economy town. It has a large hotel area surrounding a man-made lagoon at the head of the Gulf of Elat. Tourists come to Elat in large numbers to bathe in its warm sea. Elat is now far from the frontier town it had been in the early 1950s.

Index

Acknowledgments

The Publishers wish to express their appreciation to the following individuals and institutions for their help:

Ely Schiller Ariel – Publishing House; Zohar Aloufi City Archivist, Haifa City Archives; Rivka Gonen; Monica Katzman Panorama, Jerusalem; Reuven Koffler, The Central Zionist Archives, Jerusalem; Sima Selig, Photo Archives, Jewish National Fund

Illustrations:

A.A.M. van der Heyden: 60 bottom

Courtesy of Jonathan Sheink: 12

The Museum of Photography at Tel-Hai Industrial Park: 14, 15, 30 top, 34, 36 top, 40, 44, 46, 51, 63, 99, 172 top, 192 center, 250

The Central Zionist Archives, Jerusalem: 7 bottom, 8 top, 11 left and right, 19 top, 21, 24, 29, 30 left and right, bottom, 33 bottom, 48 bottom, 56 center and bottom, 60 top, 61 top, 72 top, 73, 74 bottom, 75, 87 top, 88, 95 top and center, 96 center, 106, 108, 111,112, 113 top, 121 top, 122, 126 bottom, 127 bottom, 134 top, 145 top, 150 top and bottom, 154, 155 top, 156 bottom, 160 top, 164 bottom, 166 top and bottom, 168 top, 175 top, 180, 181 top, 183, 185, 188 bottom, 190 top and center, 200 top, 203 bottom, 204 bottom, 205 top left and top right, 212 top left and bottom, 221 the first three top pictures, 224 center, 236 bottom, 249

Government Press Office: 8 bottom, 10 bottom, 22, 23 top and bottom, 33 top, 35 top, 42 bottom, 47 center, 64, 66 top, 68 top, 76, 92 top, 96 top, 105, 107 left, 109 top, 115 top, 128 center, 128 bottom, 130, 132 bottom, 133, 140 top, 141 top, 143 top,147 bottom, 152 top and bottom, 177 bottom, 178, 179, 182, 190 bottom, 195 top and bottom, 201 top, 202 bottom, 204 top, 208 top and bottom, 210 top and bottom, 212 top right, 214, 216 top, 219 center and bottom, 220 top, 221 bottom, 224 bottom, 228 top, 232, 233 top, 234 top, 235 top, 238 top, 239 top, 242 top, 244 center and bottom, 246

Jerusalem City Archives: 6, 7 top, 16, 17 top, 19 bottom, 26, 33 center, 36 center, 38, 41, 48 top, 54 top, 56 top, 67 top

The "K'han" Museum, Hadera: 101 top, 138 center and bottom

The Jerusalem Publishing House, Jerusalem: 177 top

Photo Archives, Jewish National Fund: 10 top, 71 top, 100, 101 bottom, 103, 107 top, 109 bottom, 110, 113 left, 116 top, 118 top, 120 top, 124 center and bottom, 134 center, 142 top, 144 top, 186, 202 top, 206 top, 217 top, 222 top and bottom, 224 top, 231 top and bottom, 233 left, 234 bottom, 243 top, 244 top, 251 top

Courtesy of Ely Schiller – Ariel Publishing House: 17 bottom, 18, 42 top, 52 top and center, 55 top, 58, 71 bottom, 78 top, 81 bottom, 102, 104 top and bottom, 107 bottom, 114, 119 top, 124 top, 136 top, 147 the first three top pictures, 148 top, 149 top, 154 top, 158, 160 bottom, 164 top, 176, 181 bottom, 188 top, 192 top and bottom, 196, 199 bottom, 218 bottom, 227 top, 229 top, 230, 236 top and center, 252 top and center

The Hayim Shtayer collection, Haifa: 35 center, 74 top, 117 top, 156 center, 172 bottom, 174 top

Tel Aviv City Archives: 9, 70, 72 bottom, 77 top and bottom, 82 top and bottom, 84, 90 top, 92 bottom

Nagan Barak: 28, 31, 32, 35 bottom, 37, 41 bottom, 45 top, 52 bottom, 57, 59, 61 bottom, 81 top, 90 bottom, 93, 116 bottom, 117 bottom, 131, 135 right, 136 bottom, 138 top, 165, 168 bottom, 171 top and bottom, 175 bottom

Dudu Netach: 54 bottom, 55 bottom

The Hebrew University of Jerusalem Photo Archives: 20, 50 top

Haifa City Archives: 155 bottom, 156 top, 162 top and bottom, 169, 170 top and bottom

Hayutman Family, Karkur: 135

The Council for a Beautiful Israel, Tel Aviv: 188 bottom

Typesetting and Pagination: Keterpress Enterprises Ltd., Jerusalem

Language editing and proof reading: Rachel Feldman

Secretary: Shoshana Lewis